Indoor Green

Living with Plants

Mr Kitly's Bree Claffey
Photography by Lauren Bamford

First published in Australia in 2015
by Thames & Hudson Australia Pty Ltd
11 Central Boulevard Portside Business Park
Port Melbourne Victoria 3207
ABN: 72 004 751 964

www.thameshudson.com.au

© Bree Claffey (text)
Reprinted 2016

18 17 16 15 5 4 3 2

ISBN: 9780500500538

National Library of Australia Cataloguing-in-Publication entry
Claffey, Bree, author.
Indoor Green : Living with Plants / Bree Claffey.
House plants.
House plants in interior decoration.
Indoor gardening.
Interior landscaping.
635.965

Editing: Writers Reign
Design: Darren Sylvester
Photography: Lauren Bamford
Printed and bound in China by Imago

Acknowledgements My thanks goes out to all the plant friends
featured in this book who generously welcomed us into their
spaces, shared plant knowledge and stories, and made unique and
insightful contributions. You overwhelmed me with your sheer
enthusiasm, floored me with your generosity, and so gracefully
endured endless clarifying questions such as esoteric plant names
in Japanese, how exactly one might make music from plants,
and if Himalayan salt crystals really would improve a Fiddle leaf
fig's chances. My deep thanks also to those who made elements
of this book possible and without whom it would be the poorer:
dear Yumi and Taka from Dear Plastic for their Japanese–English
translation with the lightest of touch; the one and only Karl Scullin
for the introduction to Joe and his orchids and for the help with
Joe's interview; Chonsu for her invaluable and always delightful
help with Kyoto connections; Christie of Folk Architects for the
introduction to Georgina and her Winter Garden; my good friend
Claire for the timely alert of the Titan's 2015 flowering event; Mark
at Paradisia Nursery for his specific advice on Vanda orchids and
Tillandsia care; and to Eve Archbold for casting her professional
horticultural eye over the text. Also to Paulina at Thames &
Hudson for asking me to do this book in the first place, and for
her trust and beautiful enthusiasm for all things plant-related.
My thanks to Darren Sylvester who has the greatest style and
to Lauren Bamford, photographer extraordinaire and the best
possible companion and fellow plant enthusiast in making this
book. And to Julian for everything. And finally to my dear Mum
and Dad (who also happen to be the epicentre of Mr Kitly plant
stand production) – quite simply, you two are the best.

Indoor
Green
Living
with
Plants

Thames & Hudson

Contents

Introduction

Bree Claffey

Houseplants are enduringly popular indoor companions. They have been collected, written about, arranged, and admired throughout history. One of the earliest records of a yen for cultivating plants indoors is in 1603 when British inventor and writer Hugh Plat wrote Floraes Paradise in which he suggested 'vines, apricots and plums growing on the outer house wall be allowed to wander indoors and crawl over the ceilings.'

The topic of houseplants brings to mind more than a potted plant in a corner. It encompasses the art of decorative arrangement, the romance of the past, and botanical precision – notions that are at the core of this book. My imagination is enlivened by thoughts of inspired indoor garden arrangements and verdant interior scenes. I romanticise about fern-filled Victorian-era parlours and magnificent glasshouses arching above rare palms. I pore over encyclopeadic lists of indoor species replete with Latin names and detailed notes on history and care.

Plant talk is not only the domain of long-time fans of the potted plant. A contemporary wave of houseplant appreciation is cultivating a renewed interest in all things houseplant and the various creative, social and environmental dimensions of indoor gardening are a topic of interest for many. My exploration of indoor greenery in *Indoor Green* is rooted in decor, nostalgia and botany, but also puts out new shoots and explores how houseplants can enliven discussions of creativity, aesthetics, community, culture and the environment.

In 2010 I opened my store Mr Kitly in Melbourne curating and selling houseplants and items for the home and indoor garden. My interest in arrangements of potted plants and enclosed gardens formed during the five years I lived in Japan. I first went to Japan to live in 1997 when I had just turned 21. Regular visits since have given me the chance to fully appreciate the careful consideration the Japanese give

to the pairing of pots and plants and how assiduously Japanese plant enthusiasts present and label their plants. This keen attention to detail provides a telling insight into the unique beauty of houseplant culture in that country. In 2008 on a visit to New York I observed indoor plants rampant in Brooklyn apartments, plants climbing up and down fire escapes and hanging indoor baskets for sale out the front of fruit shops. The sheer exuberance of houseplants in a highly urbanised environment and the loose and free-ranging appreciation for plant life in New York was the final prompt I needed to open my

Right: Mr Kitly triangle plant stand made by my dad with Jessica Hans ceramic planter and begonia.

Opposite: Mr Kitly's east-facing shop room provides perfect morning light for the Fiddle leaf fig and Asparagus fern.

own store and set about exploring houseplant culture in Melbourne. I drew on my admiration for both the detailed beauty of Japan and the apparent chaos of New York's indoor jungles to make Mr Kitly in Melbourne. Soon, I discovered a dedicated, thoughtful, creative and passionate community of fellow indoor gardeners.

As I've discovered, houseplants can open up new worlds. One of the most time-consuming yet interesting elements of making this book was researching the botanical histories and Latin names of each plant. I became somewhat obsessed. During this process I came across a quote from a book by novelist J. G. Ballard which seemed to encapsulate the world I found myself in: 'Plant classification was an entire universe of words; every weed in the camp had a name. Names surrounded everything; invisible encyclopedias lay in every hedge and ditch.'

My newfound obsession with esoteric Latin names made me wonder if there was a word for an all-consuming interest in indoor plants. The closest I could find was 'Pteridomania' – the British mid-19th century term for an obsession with ferns. 'Orchidelerium' was another classic example of the aristocratic interest in tropical plant collecting in Victorian Britain and Europe. Looking at what it is to be a plant

way to point to a deeper meaning of happiness.
Plants also bring happiness in their ability to
connect people. Neighbours, family, colleagues
and friends swapping plant care tips and
cuttings shows how houseplants help build
community. The world of houseplants is one of
exchange of knowledge and tips, a refreshingly
currency-free trading system. The humanist
ability of houseplants to nurture memories and
link generations is beautifully told in the types
of stories that crop up when talking plants.

For those who like to collect and to
decorate, plants are also a perennially popular
choice in interior decoration. This book
presents a unique opportunity to explore
notions of decor, and to ask deeper questions
on how and why we find aesthetic pleasure in
plants. Western traditions of aesthetic theories
sit alongside visits to Japanese shops and artists
who approach plant display from a symbolic
perspective, such as 10^{12} TERRA whose work
is influenced by traditional Japanese concepts
such as *mitate* which is the art of arranging
flowers and plants to convey a fable or
landscape. Both provide interesting insight into
these questions.

Plants have a positive effect on our
environment and wellbeing. Experts have
examined the therapeutic benefits of plants
and studies have shown they reduce stress in
working environments and produce tangible
wellbeing outcomes for people in hospitals
and offices. In one of the book's essays, Dr BC
Wolverton's highly influential research explores
the efficacy of plants as air filters – research
that continues to open up potential for cleaner
buildings and environments.

Plants not only filter the air but also the
mind. Houseplants are contained nature
selected for their ability to grow inside and
discussion of nature comes up again and again
in the book when considering why houseplants
are so adored. In the plant visits, many people
speak about a strong sense of a connection to
nature and the connection to the cycle of life
which having potted plants inside brings.

Finally, I am very interested in the role plants
can play in artistic impulse and creativity.
Many of the plant visits in this book are
centered on creative practice, and one of the
most satisfying elements of Mr Kitly is working
with artists who work with plants in new
and interesting ways. The first collaborative
project we did was with ceramicist Bridget
Bodenham to create a unique ceramic

collector today, orchid grower Joe Crawford,
who we meet in the book, is a splendid example
of how a plant collection can become a lifelong
endeavour that enriches the spirit.

As many of the stories in this book
demonstrate, caring for plants can be a deeply
enriching and reflective activity. Small daily
rituals like watering your plants and examining
their leaves provide a quiet contemplative
moment. On face value we live in rather
a manic consumerist society – one where
the production of desires via marketing
can sometimes leave little space for quiet
contemplation, silence and imperfection. A life
lived with plants might help in its own small

planter. I find constant inspiration in the work of photographers, potters, artists and craftspeople whose creative output strays into the world of plants. This sits alongside the very essential tenet that to actively create an indoor garden and to collect and care for houseplants is an inherently creative endeavor. I believe there is mystery and magic in this relationship.

I hope this book captures a little of the 'romance' of houseplants. As you'll discover, this extends from visits to a glasshouse to the enchantment of European indoor 'winter gardens' like Georgina Nagy's Hungarian Winter Garden to the intrigue of discovering lost or forgotten species like the Chinese money plant. *Indoor Green* is not concerned with prescribing how-to tips, or telling you how to make your house and plants look. I hope that by combining essays about how houseplants play a part in aesthetics through to science; interviews that illuminate individual approaches to life with plants; and plant care and botanical histories of plant specimens, I might pique curiosity and inspire further reconnaissance.

I would be overjoyed if you felt impelled to go to the museum to see a Henri Rousseau or David Hockney painting after reading the interviews with Paul Wackers and Emily Ferretti. Or if you were motivated to talk to your body corporate about new ways to use plants in your apartment block like the residents of The Beverley Hills apartments. Or simply felt the need to contemplate the houseplants in your life with renewed attention. Plants are gorgeous, multifarious, messy and real and can inspire all kinds of action and reflection. *Indoor Green* is an invitation to potter around and ponder ideas with a watering can in hand enjoying a life lived with plants.

See more of Bree Claffey's world of indoor green at her shop and gallery at mrkitly.com.au

Plant
visits

Indoor green

Location
Tokyo, Japan
Residents
Noriko Konuma,
Tomoyasu Konuma
and their teenage children
Hikari and Shieru
Occupations
Noriko: curator;
Tomoyasu: urushi lacquer artist
Place
Home and studio
Plant density
Medium
Light
Bright
Plant list
Guiana chestnut
Madagascar dragon tree
Philodendron selloum
Flamingo flower
Pony tail palm
Blueberry
Morning glory

Noriko, Tomoyasu and their children live in a quiet outer suburb about one hour by train from the centre of Tokyo. They designed their house and studio themselves. Noriko studied art curatorship in England before returning to the Tokyo art world where she is the curator and CEO of Tokyo creative space KUMU. Tomoyasu is a highly respected artist in the traditional craft of urushi lacquerware. Noriko is a good friend of Mr Kitly's favourite designer Masanori Oji and I met Noriko when visiting Oji-san in Tokyo. Tomoyasu answered the questions about the plants in their home, as he is the plant lover in the family. During our interview Noriko used the words 'indoor green', a common term in Japan used to describe having plants inside. It is an apt description of the beautiful plant world the Konuma family has created.

Could you describe your home?
I am a woodcrafter and so I needed a studio at home. The ground floor is my studio and the second floor my home. I designed this house with a conscious connection between the outside and inside. It is a house where you feel the wind, light and rain when inside. One section of the house where we grow many plants has a glass roof and this creates a feeling of an inside garden.

Which was your first plant?
It was a Morning glory plant. In Japan everyone in Year 1 grows a Morning glory plant from seed. This was my first experience of the joy of growing plants. Over many years I kept replanting the seeds I took from the flowers and watched the flowers grow. This is where I learnt different skills like staking when growing plants.

The skylight and natural light in your home is beautiful. Did the architecture of your home inform or lead to the presence of so many wonderful plants, or was it a collaboration or partnership between a love of plants/indoor green and the new architecture?
I am always conscious of where plants are placed. To say that we designed the house

around our plants is a little over the top but plants are naturally part of our lives and so the space is naturally conscious of our plants. Having natural light or wind is not only important for plants but also for human beings. Sometimes we even see the light of the moon cast shadows of our plants onto the floor.

Do you have any special tips on taking care of plants? Yours all look so happy and healthy.
Caring for and talking to them. When I give them water or look after them I always think positive thoughts from the bottom of my heart. Our plants normally grow very big. I sometimes ask them 'Do you think you could grow smaller?' but our plants never listen to this request! When I am busy and don't have time to talk to them they lose energy straight away.

What is your general approach to plant care?
I think it's most important to help plants adapt to the environment in which they are placed. For example, if it's hot or cold outside I do not keep the inside temperature always the same. If it is very hot and dry outside, I only give the minimum amount of water to the plant. During this time I have created a difficult

Opposite: Urushi lacquerware bowls by Tomoyasu in the dining space as well as a Philodendron selloum and a blueberry bought for their oldest daughter for her primary school graduation. Blueberry plants need very good light to survive indoors. Their daughter is now in Year 12 so this is an exceptional specimen.

environment for the plant but I keep talking to it with encouraging words so it doesn't mind being in the space. I am trying to encourage the plant to become independent. It is strict but at the same time enjoyable for the plant, similar to having children. If they fall weak, I will help them with my whole being. If plants can adapt to an environment, they can be left on their own.

How did you learn to take care of plants?
I learnt the basics from childhood experiences and just trial and error. When there is something that I don't know I will look it up in a book, but to tell the truth every plant changes depending on the condition or place, so these answers are not always reliable. I think everyone has a green thumb. The difference is whether you are conscious of this or not. It is not that I have special powers, it is just that I try to help plants grow.

Do you think indoor plants are 'back in fashion'? Did they ever go out of fashion in Tokyo?
To have plants in your life is something very natural and will always be popular.

How do you think having plants in your home impacts on your life?
When there are plants, the *Ki (Qi)* flows well. *Ki* is about life force, natural energy and its flow. When I think of space I am always considering how well the *Ki* will flow. Plants play an important role in creating the good flow of this natural energy in a space.

Do you have any plants that are extra special to you?
There are many plants that we bought when we first married that are very big now. Those can be seen in some of the photos taken of our house. They were very small at first, planted in cup-sized planters. They were tiny plants that you wouldn't even notice in a 'green shop' (plant shop). Now they have been replanted into very large planters, so big that I cannot lift them on my own. These plants have become part of our lives, something that we have a very deep attachment to.

Can you imagine a life without plants?
That is difficult. Even in a small space, I think of growing some kind of plant. The exchange of energy between a plant and myself is crucial. I cannot explain this well but when I have plants around I do not feel alone. I feel more connected and at one with the universe.

The imaginary plant

Location
Northcote, Melbourne, Australia
Resident
Emily Ferretti
Occupation
Artist
Place
Studio
Plant density
Low
Light
Indirect bright

Emily Ferretti's painting studio is in a shared artist warehouse in a northern suburb in Melbourne. It's a relatively utilitarian modern building presenting a non-committal brick facade to the street. Emily's space is a coveted large front studio with the factory windows that provide the indirect natural light essential for a painter. The light is subtle in Emily's studio and the actual plants there are somewhat melancholy. I admire Emily's poetic paintings of pot plants and daily ephemera; so this interview is not so much about a plant devotee but about the role plants play in her work. Emily's still life paintings can strongly convey what it means to be human and her connection between art and plants is fascinating to explore.

Why do you use pot plants in your paintings?
I started using plants in my paintings as a way to push the abstraction in my work. I was interested in the way plants can cut in or out of a scene obstructing and covering parts of the picture, filling spaces in a dynamic way. They also bring homeness to an image and can convey a myriad of emotions depending on how they are painted. They are versatile and that's exciting when you have ideas you want to flesh out.

Would you describe your plant still lifes as a portrait of a plant or do they move beyond that?
I have never been interested in just painting as a way to describe reality. There needs to be something more magical that happens. I want there to be an essence or mood that goes along with it. The beauty of the plant is that it can be abstracted and manipulated a lot more than inorganic objects. You can push the limits of a plant's character by changing its mood through shape and palette.

Still life painting is a way to portray the quiet, fleeting moments of everyday life. Does a plant subject particularly enhance this feeling?
I think so. As the words suggest, the 'still life' is a very reflective way to capture a moment in time. I feel a still life can be very sad as well. An object that stands alone can often be very loaded with melancholy. Often in my paintings I find that if I place a plant (that is organic and living) next to an inanimate object, there is an automatic activation of the emotional duality in the work. I think this activation is the same reason humans get so much pleasure in having plants in their living spaces.

The pot plant vessels often take on a life of their own in your pictures. The 'Imaginary Plant' series has some beautifully detailed vessels. How do vessel and plant relate in your paintings?
Often the vessels became devices that helped ground the plants into a specific reality or mood. A lot of the vessels became an extension of the plants, or in some cases became very understated. They became another way to play around with form and abstraction. It is always interesting to see the plant's juxtaposition with the vessel and the way they inform one another.

Is there ever a connection between your chosen colour palette and the colour of a plant subject?
There is always a bouncing off that happens from colour to colour. Occasionally a plant does dictate the sort of colour I use but because the images are not based on reality, there is also a freedom to think outside of a naturalistic palette. It's my own visual language, so if I want to put a blue leaf next to a green one I do.

Opposite: *Table with Plant* (detail), 2013, oil on linen. Photo by Jeremy Dillion.

Are there other artists whose work references houseplants you admire?
An obvious answer is David Hockney. Hockney's still life and scene drawings have been very influential. I think he is a technical master and a great example of an artist who has taken inspiration in the everyday things around him to form unique and highly engaging images. His classic California plants can be seen making appearances in a lot of his early work. A younger artist whose work I also engage with is Jonas Wood. He is also a Californian artist who has plants feature in most of his work in some way or another. His paintings are flat and more graphic but amazingly detailed and inventive. His wife is also an artist (Shio Kusaka) and she makes a lot of the pots that feature in his paintings.

What are your thoughts on why plants so often make their appearance in art, and how nature can inspire?
I think nature is inspirational because it is living and bigger than us. I really love plants but I am totally blown away when I am walking through a forest of established trees. The scale and time that has passed through them makes it an unstoppable emotional force.

There is a sense of nostalgia and sentimentality at times around pot plants. Do you personally have any particular emotional connections to your plants?
I think this is very personal. If there is a story behind the plant or it has some significance I think it would be heartless not to want to cherish and feel a connection to that. Saying this I think plants have become a design feature and some people have little connection with them, beyond their beauty and form. This isn't necessarily a negative thing as a lot of our possessions start as strangers in our rooms. I think these connections take time. For example, I have this plant in my bathroom that I originally just bought because it was hardy, easy to maintain and interesting. I started off with very little connection to it but I would look at it very closely every day in the shower. A few weeks ago it sprouted one very beautiful white flower over night. It was such a moment of connection for me. I felt privileged to have watched its evolution and now an emotional narrative has formed.

Above: Emily's studio is relatively bare of real plants because she often gets so distracted by her work that they rarely get watered.

Opposite, top: Installation view of the series 'Imaginary Plant' at Sophie Gannon Gallery. Photo by Matthew Stanton.

The art of brass

Location
Melbourne CBD, Australia
Resident
Anna Varendorff
Occupation
Jeweller, artist
Place
Studio
Plant density
Medium
Light level
Bright direct to
Indirect bright
Plant list
Parlour palm
Peace lily
Begonia
Pot belly fig
Airplant
Maidenhair fern
Rubber plant
Succulents (various)
Rope hoya

Anna Varendorff occupies a small studio on the fifth floor of the Nicholas Building, a 1920s building in the Melbourne CBD with a long history of housing artist studios. She has a background in jewellery, but now works more often on the creation of brass objects. Anna has collaborated with Mr Kitly many times over the years on plant-based artworks, including delicate brass plant hangers called 'plant necklaces' and small brass table top 'plant props'. Anna's instinctively sculptural approach to function and support in her plant-based work is fascinating. This approach paired with working in brass, a nice aesthetic fit with indoor green, makes for a perfect partnership with plants.

Can you tell me a little about the houseplants in your studio?
The plants in my studio are very loved, but I'm not naturally a green thumb. My dear friend Isobel gave the beautiful hoya to me, and the Peace lilies are from my partner Haima. My friend Kate gave me the airplant, and we each bought a Rubber plant from Mr Kitly the same afternoon. Lots of the green leafy chaps here have arrived from friends.

You have made some really beautiful pieces related to houseplants for Mr Kitly over the years. Can you tell me about your work process when you get these plant-based requests?
I have made plant-related pieces specifically for Mr Kitly over the years, because I love the space and am super drawn to its aesthetic. I made the plant necklaces and plant props very spontaneously, as a simple gesture to support the indoor plants I knew or imagined might need a little structural support, as mine are a delicate brood. The objects I make to support and elevate planted pots come simply from thinking about how I could best make a brass structure, which could have a moment of 'exchange' with the plant it was working with. A similar ideology to the brass objects

I make within my sculptural work that offer opportunity for exchange with the audience. These thoughts stem from my thinking as a jeweller. I still love all of the pieces I have made for plants over the years, as these objects come from a functional need and so remain useful.

Do you have particular plants in mind when making your plant necklaces and plant props?
Well for the plant necklaces I think of Maidenhair – which I struggle to grow but I really love. It is such a fuzzy bundle at the end of the chain. And for the plant props I think of my hoya and its long arms, and holding them off the ground as it grows.

You work mostly in brass. What are your thoughts on how brass and greenery work together?
I think the combination is magical and very natural. The plant pieces I made in brass precede my knowledge of other plant objects and yet the pairing of plants and brass is very old. The green of the plants and the warm gold of the brass look so beautiful together. Also the physical strength of the material and the way I can solder it together means that the brass can look delicate while being strong. In this way it is delicate and unobtrusive – a beautiful detail.

Opposite: 'Brass Free Object' hanging in Anna's studio.

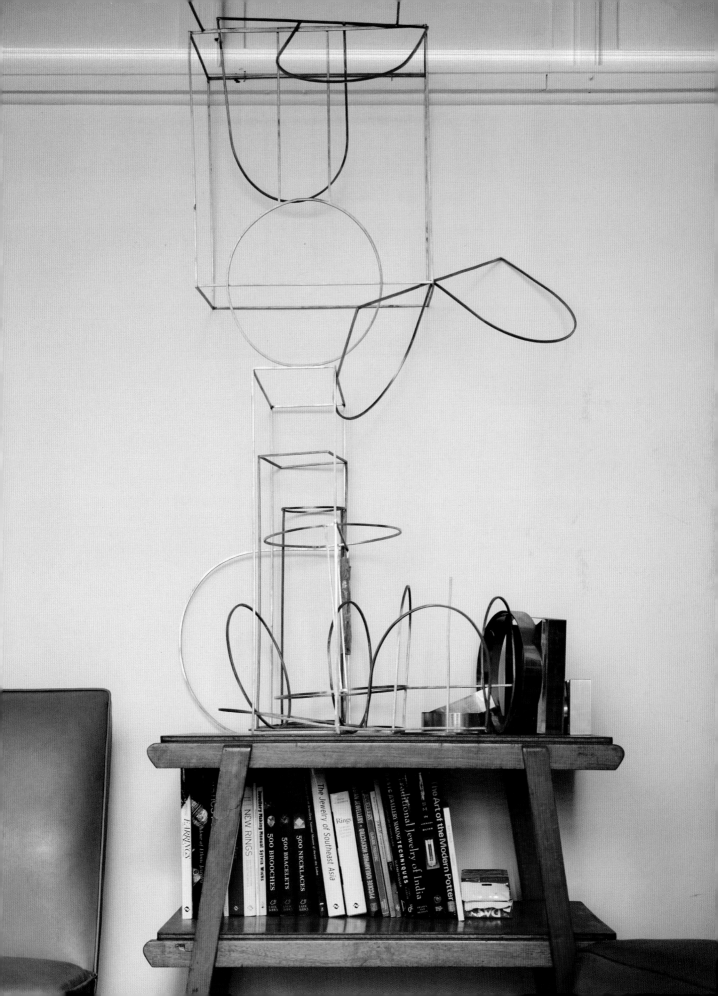

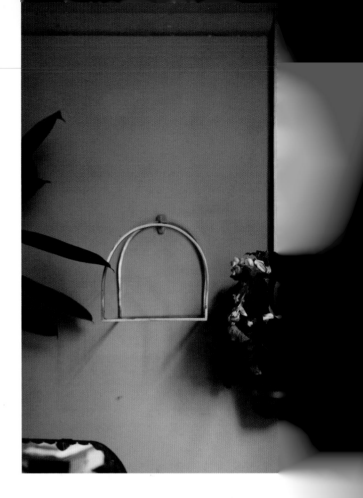

What is your top houseplant tip?
My top tip is to collect the cold water as your shower is warming up and to distribute that to your houseplants. That way the plants get a little water regularly and less water escapes use.

You recently visited Japan for the first time. Was that visit inspiring for your plant-based artworks?
Yes, after I had made my plant prop pieces I heard about the Japanese plant supports that have historically supported ageing, weighty trees against gravity all over Japan. This prompted my first trip to Japan and when I was there I was totally enamoured with the simple, thoughtful and resourceful props that supported trees everywhere I went. These props were mostly wood, and their material sympathy with the branches which they prop makes for gentle intertwining of woods, wrapping and moulding into each other. This has caused me to rethink my adherence to the use of metals as my primary working material, and more towards considering materials that, by their nature, have a poetic rapport with the function of the object I am considering.

Top: A begonia hangs in Anna's brass plant hanger, which was made for a Mr Kitly and MONA collaboration.

Bottom: A Parlour palm suspended in one of Anna's 'plant necklaces' made for Mr Kitly's 'Planted' gallery show in 2012.

Opposite, top: Anna's small-scale plant props, including a tiny but perfect support for an airplant (far right), allow for airflow. The opaque glass offers the fern and the airplant protection from very bright light. Contrary to popular belief, some succulents require protection from direct sun. The one on the left can tolerate more direct light, but is happy enough under these light conditions.

Opposite, bottom (L-R): Parlour palm, succulents, Pot belly fig, Peace lily and Rope hoya.

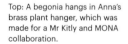

Kyoto potted garden

Location
Kyoto, Japan
Resident
Miho Tanaka
Occupation
Plant shop owner
Place
Shop
Plant density
High
Light level
Bright
(potted plants outside shop)
and indirect bright
(plants inside shop)
Plant list
Succulent 'kokedama'
(moss balls)
Japanese maple
Rosemary
Heavenly bamboo
Thistle
Japanese winterberry
Corkscrew water rush
Guiana chestnut
Albuca
Green penny fern
Japanese wind orchid
Juniper tree
Japanese clover
Japanese felt fern
Hare's foot fern
Pearl orchid
Poppy

Miho Tanaka owns a plant shop in the back streets of the Higashiyama hills in Eastern Kyoto. At first Miho sold plants and coffee, nowadays she only sells plants. Miho does not just sell houseplants. Her shop is an example of the quintessentially Japanese potted garden where inside and outside meet, with potted plants displayed on the street close to the doorstep of houses and in other urban corners. I first came across Miho's shop when I was living and working in Kyoto. It appeared to me as a hidden wonderland of plants. Miho's shop has been a strong aesthetic memory and inspiration for me since leaving Japan. The sense of detail in Miho's shop matches Miho's connection to the plants .

How did you learn about plants?
My parents were selling plants so I learnt by helping them out, reading books, and sometimes I learnt from the customers.

Could you tell me about your initial combination of plants and coffee?
In high school I worked in a café and the café owner became my mentor. This was an important period in my life. I learnt about music, art and life – he taught me many things. I developed my aesthetics and values during this time. He became a coffee roaster. Then I decided to create a shop with plants and coffee. I thought it would be cool to combine plants and coffee. To speak frankly, I didn't have the passion or interest I have towards my plants with the coffee. The world of coffee, like plants, is not something to be taken lightly or is easily done. So I decided to just focus on plants.

Why did you decide to open Miho Tanaka's Plant Shop?
My mentor taught me the importance of women to have their own work. With this in mind I decided not to work for some company. I was interested in my family's plant business but I wanted to find a way of showing and selling plants on my own. I have been running my shop for eleven years now.

What do you love about plants? Do you have many houseplants at home?
The naturally occurring shapes, the shapes that have meaning and purpose. This is what I like. I do not have many plants at home. Many customers think that I live with a lot of plants, but I only have a few succulents and rosemary.

You have many tiny bonsai planters in your shop. I am curious, would you call bonsai an indoor plant?
I do not consider bonsai an indoor plant. I think of indoor plants as plants that will grow healthy indoors. Bonsai are usually plants that are grown outdoors. They are plants for you to enjoy seasonal changes, autumnal leaves or fruits. It is about growing larger natural shapes in a small planter. The planter and plant take on a new shape. It is about recreating a new world within a small space. It would be beautiful to have indoors but very difficult to grow.

Most visitors to Japan love the potted gardens everywhere. In Australia if we did this, the plants would likely get stolen! Why do you think so many people make potted gardens here in Kyoto?
Firstly, people own very little land. Customers from other prefectures have also commented on the amount of potted gardens in Kyoto. I always thought 'Really?' but I guess there are a

Opposite: Miho Tanaka's 'potted garden' is quintessentially Kyoto and includes many typically Japanese species, rarely available elsewhere.

lot. I also place potted plants outside the street of our shop. Sometimes these plants do get stolen, but I also have this in mind when I place them outside.

What's the best piece of advice on plants you have received and from whom?
My plant farmer, who is an old man. This old man would greet me every time I went there. He would say, *'You ki ta na'* (good for coming!). He is a master at propagating from cuttings (grafting and rooting). While doing his work he would say 'Always have your antennas up.' Everyday new things are being made. Don't just focus on traditional ways of doing things. Be open to all the good things. It is important to believe in the things you think are good, even though others may not, but it is also important to see good in the things that are outside of what you know.

I hear you have done some plant installations in Tokyo. Could you describe any of these for me?
In Hayama, a gallery called 'Arahabaki' invited me to hold an exhibition. This show was called 'Tanaka Miho *ni yori sotte*' ('Together with Tanaka Miho'). Many artists created works based around plants. Each artwork was paired with a plant. It was a very special space but I was troubled by it. I wanted to sell plants suited for outdoors. Their shape, colour and appearance

were so beautiful and they worked well indoors against a white wall. I tell my customers who buy these plants to please grow them outside. I tell them to grow a few plants outside and constantly rotate with one plant indoors.

What are your top three tips on taking care of plants indoors?
1. If you are not good at giving water, place your plant next to a tap; 2. As your plant won't get rainwater or morning dew, please spray water on the leaves; 3. Observe the plant daily!

What are some of your favourite plants?
My favourites are ferns and moss and also thistles. I like flowers that have a long stem. I also like poppies.

What plans and hopes do you have for the future of Miho Tanaka's Plant Shop?
There are many things I want to do. I have never sold cut flowers but lately I have become interested in them and am thinking that maybe I want to have some in the shop. I have created bouquets and headpieces for weddings in the past and I would like to do more of this. I would also like to do some gardening work. I would like to organise a dried flower/plant exhibition. While selling living, cut and dried flowers and plants, I want to continue expressing the ideas I have towards plants.

Above: Miho's shop is full of many unusual plants, small pots and planters.

A suitable muse

Location
Brooklyn, New York,
United States
Resident
Paul Wackers
Occupation
Artist
Place
Studio
Plant density
High
Light level
Indirect bright
Plant list
Shamrock plant
Spiderwort
Bromeliad
Rubber plant
Airplant
Cornstalk plant
Fiddle leaf fig
Asparagus fern
Aloe vera
Succulents (various)

Paul Wackers is an artist who paints, draws and, more recently, does ceramic work. His studio is in an industrial area of Williamsburg in Brooklyn. The two walls of windows provide consistent light throughout the day – good for painting and for plants. Paul has collaborated with Mr Kitly ceramic artist Jessica Hans, and his studio is peppered with familiar ceramic pieces by artists we both admire. Paul's paintings often begin from a small incidental object arrangement. The final piece might appear to be fantastical but maintains its real life roots. The layered jungle-like plant world in his studio may also seem somewhat whimsical but Paul's plant collection clearly has its roots in the real world.

Can you describe your studio?
The building itself is almost all artist studios or arts-related businesses. When I saw this space I was moving out of a shared studio that had no windows, I instantly fell in love with it. My studio is a corner spot, so I have two walls of windows – one to the north and the other to the east. It is pretty perfect for a painting studio since I never have intense direct light except for a few moments very early in the day, and the light level and quality stays pretty consistent throughout the day. With any space I take over the first thing I bring to it is a few plants. I just need them around, they soften and help a place have life.

How do plants contribute to your creative space?
They are very inspiring to have around as they offer natural and unexpected ways of finding lines and shapes that are easily translated into paintings and drawings. I am also very drawn to the never-ending variations to be found among them, be it leaf shape or lack of leaves to colours and textures. And then if they bloom that is a whole other rollercoaster ride. They are endlessly fascinating studio mates.

Which plant here is the longest occupant and can you tell me a little about its history?
I think the one that has been with me the longest is the shamrock. I have not found a

way to kill it yet. Bone dry and a good soak with water will bring new sprouts and flowers. I think I originally got the cutting from a friend fifteen or sixteen years ago and it has or parts of it have been with me in three cities. It's not the most impressive but it has seen it all.

How do you manage plant maintenance with so many plants to look after? How much time every day do you spend taking care of your plants?
I really don't spend all that much time tending to them. I just give them water when they look a little sad or tired. Then if things need a trim I do it. Or if they're looking a little dusty I clean the leaves real quick. But the one thing I do that is maybe different is just mist the plants with a spray bottle from time to time between watering which I think helps relieve the stresses they may have being inside in the city. I think it makes them happy.

Any special tips on plant care?
I would say my sprayer technique. I also think just looking at them is important. It's nice to have them but if you don't know what they look like you will miss the signs that they are not happy. See how the leaves change in light and heat, or cold or dry or wet. It can be very revealing to take a moment every day and see what is going on. I use my Fiddle leaf fig as a barometer for when

to water. When those big leaves are hanging low it's time to water every one. If the plant is holding its leaves up tall, things are just fine. Also don't get too beat up over a loss.

What techniques do you use for suspending plants?
My friend Kellie made a bunch of the macramé hangers for me and I got a few as gifts, but it's just all hung up on some cord across the corner. Nothing special, it's what I had that worked out at the moment.

Do you have a favourite plant here?
I really like the bromeliads, they just have the most exciting flowers. And when they flower it seems never-ending.

What is your ultimate artwork involving houseplants?
I think if I had an Alex Katz painting of trees I could never leave the house again. Staring at those paintings is so satisfying. Or perhaps a Rousseau jungle painting would be amazing.

How have plants made their way into your work?
Plants are a pretty key part of my paintings. I think since they are often very clearly kept plants and not wild they stand for a human presence in my work. I also think they have a way of allowing some very unexpected shapes and lines to come into play in a composition.

What came first? So many plants making their way into your studio, or plants making their way into your paintings?
I think I could not resist using plants in my life as my subjects. I find them very satisfying and suitable muses.

Above: The great light in Paul's studio allows for a broad range of plant life. His improvised hanging garden is a nice fit with an eclectic ceramics collection.

Opposite, bottom left: A species of Asparagus fern (an invasive plant in the wild) alongside pots by Jessica Hans.

Plant music

Dylan Martorell

The role of plants in art rarely takes as literal a form than in artist and musician Dylan Martorell's creative practice. Dylan makes plant-based musical scores inspired by botanical growth. His plant instrument installations can include DIY electronics, potatoes stitched through with audio wires, a drum vibrating with water plants, or a gourd with an embedded speaker. Here Dylan discusses where botany and art meet in a collaboration between people and plants.

I discovered *The Secret Life of Plants* by Peter Tompkins and Christopher Bird on my Dad's bookshelf when I was a teenager, so I think I was primed for a future world of sentient plant life. The idea that you can create environments that grow and evolve are ideas from the plant world. The micro versus macro nature of plant structure where small simple elements following simple algorithms can evolve into large complex systems is a concept that informs everything I do in my various practices, especially music.

My background is as an improvising musician and in an attempt to break from an improvised way of creating music I aimed to create a more structural methodology. I based this methodology on elegant plant-based patterns found within my local environment. The hope was that these elegant structures would equate to elegant sound. By elegant I mean very simple patterns utilising various geometric and structural elements such as symmetry.

My form of plant music involves using the basic structural patterns of plant growth to inform the creation of music scores. The structures are chosen from details of local plants that have defined geometric growth structures, patterns set by nature. These plant structures are then mapped in a way so that the music progresses on the vertical scale that represents time. In this way you can imagine the plant growing as the music progresses. The horizontal axis represents a measure of sound, initially represented through hertz frequencies. More recently I have graphed out the horizontal axis to represent various keyboards such as church organs, harmoniums and synthesisers so that they can be translated, recorded and played live by musicians.

Everything is made of atoms and is vibrating and creating sound, so there are also various ways of theoretically using plants to create sound directly. You could use plants as conductive triggers in the house to control your lighting system, turn on the coffee machine, trigger the watering system, take a video of your cat. Anything that is conductive such as plants, metal and fluids can be used to complete a DIY electrical circuit to send a signal to a laptop. You could have wires or a sensor embedded in the soil and listen to it reacting to various changes in its environment such as moisture and heat. You could also use a contact microphone powerful enough to listen to sub-audible sounds such as the roots of the plants displacing grains of dirt.

I like the vastly different perception of time that dealing with plants gives you. Working with plants and music in a gallery offers a space where you can experiment with durational activities on a very small scale. You can create pieces of music that evolve over a month or you can create small ecosystems that have to be looked after and can often react unpredictably. One exhibition with drums full of water plants had a mosquito outbreak, which was disastrous in such a small exhibition space. After a bit of research at the local aquarium I found out that the zebra fish which inhabited the pond behind my local shopping mall would eat the mosquito larvae. After introducing the fish, the mosquito problem disappeared within 24 hours. Plants in galleries used in art works are common these days and that's a great thing as it's one step removed from creating decor for art patrons and one step closer to working with messy, unpredictable real life experience.

You can listen to Dylan's musical scores at dylanmartorell.bandcamp.com

Plant-based music score by
Dylan Martorell.

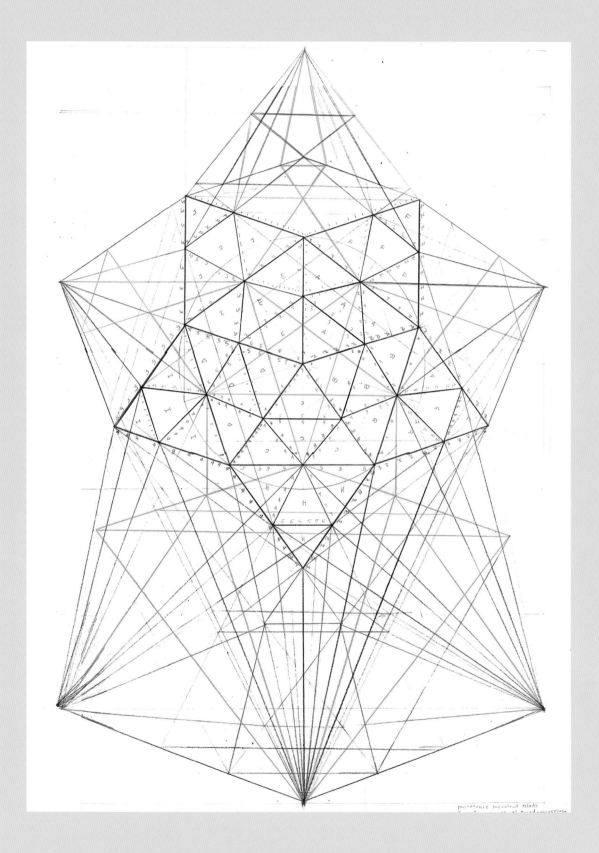

pentatonic succulent triads

A Hungarian Winter Garden

Location
Windsor, Melbourne, Australia
Resident
Georgina Nagy
Occupation
Music teacher
Place
Home
Plant density
High
Light level
Bright to indirect bright
Plant list
Begonia
Cymbidium orchid
Spider plant
Camellia
Pelargonium
Hydrangea
Mother-in-law's tongue
Pony tail palm
Spanish moss
Fruit salad plant
Chinese evergreen
Christmas cactus
Miniature grape ivy
Nasturtium
Spiderwort
Imperial green philodendron
English ivy
African violet
Syngonium

Georgina Nagy's family came from Hungary in 1950 and moved to the Melbourne inner-city suburb of Windsor in 1964 where Georgina was born. Georgina returned to Budapest in her youth to complete her music degree but has lived in her family home and taught music in Melbourne ever since. Georgina's house is an early 20th century suburban home and is filled with light and plants. There is a conservatory-like extension at the rear of the house, referred to as the 'Winter Garden', a cross between a tiled sunroom, a conservatory and an enclosed outdoor kitchen. I was introduced to Georgina by Melbourne architects and houseplant fans, Folk Architects. While working on a project next door, they visited Georgina's house and took a picture of her Mum in the middle of an oasis of indoor plants. Georgina's Mum has since passed away and this plant story is about a love of plants that spans generations and a Winter Garden alive with memories.

What is the history of Winter Gardens in Hungary?
In Hungarian we say *'Teli kert'. Kert* is garden, *teli* is winter. I think that in the country most houses had an enclosed porch where they could have plants from early spring to very late autumn, bearing in mind that the winters can be quite bitter in Hungary.

Who was the plant collector, you or your Mum?
Both of us. We were blessed with green fingers so whatever we put down just sort of took off. I repot and then I make a whole lot of little ones. I am forever giving stuff to people and I've got pot plants in my office at work and everywhere else.

The plants here are all so healthy. Can you give any insight as to why?
I think it has to do with aspect, the air and the light – they just like it. We get full morning sun across here and then a bit of afternoon sun. Everything just takes off like a rocket. The Monstera I've got upstairs in a room with the same aspect has reached the ceiling.

I can see you are propagating. What plants do you propagate regularly?
We had a huge Monstera along here and Mum said, 'No more!' We cut it up and propagated it. The pelargoniums are another one I propagate. When that flowers it's all a mass of flowers, but it has to be cut back of course. Then I propagate using the cuttings.

Do the camellias flower inside?
They most certainly do! We have the two big camellia trees and they are always a mass of flowers.

Having a planted garden inside your home brings nature very close. Has that connection been important to you?
I think everyone needs to garden. I feel unwell if I have not been able to garden for a very long time. Even if I am very tired, often mentally very tired, I need to work with the soil and work with plants. After this I will come in bone tired physically, but my mother always said the same thing – 'You've now got colour in your face.' I just need that connection.

Opposite: Georgina's Winter Garden faces north-east and is protected from strong summer sun by a shade cloth, allowing a broad range of indoor plants and plantings to grow.

Above, left: A magnificent begonia in a hanging basket.

Above, right: Detail of a tiled garden bed with a Spider plant and a Spiderwort.

Opposite, left: A large imperial green philodendron.

Opposite, right: A syngonium twining up a steel support.

Here you are semi-outdoors so you would get humidity from the air, which must help these plants?
It helps them but it also means that they are prone to fungal diseases and if you get some kind of a bug that gets in, it takes off like a rocket. We had these hopping green things that attacked both camellias a few years ago that was horrible. Beautiful lime green things they were but they would chew everything! Occasionally we will get caterpillars that will also chew everything.

What pest control methods do you use?
Every now and again I spray. I try and keep it as natural as possible. Now I've got a natural product I buy online called Miracle Soap. You can use it for just about anything, including washing your hair. We used to get a lot of problems with the hibiscus and Mum sprayed it with anything and everything but it was constantly getting this black sooty fungus. Since I've sprayed it with Miracle Soap the fungus is gone and it has massive flowers. I use it for whitefly. It also feeds the plants with magnesium and they seem to like it. Whitefly and ants bring about fungus and stickiness, that's the problem. So you need to break that cycle.

Begonias are the stars in this Winter Garden. I find they are hard to keep happy inside. What are your begonia tips?

Mum always liked the begonia with the stalks and delicate little flowers. Begonias should work for you indoors as long as they get morning sun, but not much sun. They need the sun to flower. If they are potted, they don't like to have their feet soaking in water. They like humidity so you can put pebbles into the saucer plate and put water in that and then sit it on top.

Do you have any other tips for unusual or forgotten indoor plants?

African violets should work for you inside too. Morning sun is probably the best for them, not strong light. You can have them in a fish bowl and they will take off. I used to have a big fish tank in the front room but I got sick of the cleaning maintenance. So I put charcoal in the bottom to keep it sweet and soil on top and then I put three African violets in it. The whole thing filled up with African violets and they always flowered.

Aussie burbs modernist

Location
Geelong, Australia
Residents
Andrea Shaw,
Duncan Russell-Smith,
Tilly (dog)
Occupations
Andrea: multidisciplinary
artist and designer;
Duncan: furniture maker
Place
Home
Plant density
Medium
Light level
Indirect bright
Plant list
Chain of hearts
Rubber plant
Fruit salad plant
Calathea insignia
Palms
Madagascar dragon tree
Devil's ivy
Hoya
Boston fern
Aeonium
Fiddle leaf fig
Zebra plant
Prayer plant
Lady palm
Kentia palm
Moreton Bay Chestnut
Bromeliad

Andrea, Duncan and Tilly, the dog, live in a detached 1960s brick house in the port city of Geelong in Victoria. When asked how she would describe the house Andrea calls it 'Aussie burbs modernist'. Andrea has a background in textile design but is a multidisciplinary artist creating wonders across all kinds of materials, and always with a close eye on nature and sustainability. Mr Kitly stocks Andrea's macramé plant hangers, which were inspired by Andrea's mum's stockpile of jute from the 1970s. Andrea's love of nature, as exemplified in both her art and any spare time spent outdoors surfing, is an interesting complement to her indoor plant life.

The 1960s architecture of your house just seems to match houseplants so well. Did your houseplant collection grow or change after moving here?
It most definitely grew after moving into this house. It probably grew by about a third I'd say! There are lots of little details for objects or plant placement in the stone and brick walls – not enough houses have features like this. The beautiful stone wall in the dining room has a ledge made for plants and the light in there is great also.

Who takes care of the plants?
We both do. I probably know where they are at in terms of their watering and feeding more than Duncan but he will water and mist them if they're looking droopy. He talks to them and dusts their leaves more than I do. It's probably more important to keep plants happy than we realise!

Any special tips on plant care?
We aren't plant experts by any means but we don't lose many at all (only a couple over the years). So a little fertiliser every couple of months, weekly watering (not overloading them though) and a mist for ferns and more tropical plants, music, light and some directed special attention every now and then seems to keep plants thriving.

Do you have a favourite plant?
I really like our Rubber plant for its beautifully patterned leaves (I am pattern obsessed) and its hardiness.

Is there a place in your house that you find houseplants really love?
Most of the varieties we have seem to be quite happy in the very well lit dining room. I've moved our Fiddle leaf fig around a lot as it has been really fussy. It has been happiest in the bedroom with filtered light but recently we placed a Himalayan salt lamp underneath it and it's taken off! So much new growth. Apparently plants like salt crystals.

Do you have any favourite vessels or planters to house your plant life?
I love our blue spotty Bridget Bodenham planter best. It's one of a few lovely pieces we own of Bridget's that I have traded with her over the past few years. It houses a very happy little Zebra plant.

We first met when Mr Kitly started stocking your macramé plant hangers and fassett stem vessels. Both of these are really geared around plant life but your background is in textiles. What drew you to plant-related works?

Opposite (L-R): Andrea's plant line-up includes Fruit salad plant, Lady palm, aeonium, Rubber plant, Boston fern, Zebra plant, Moreton Bay chestnut and Prayer plant. A hardy Chain of hearts also trails from the nook in the wall.

Above: Devil's ivy, hoya and Boston fern are perfect for the humid conditions of the bathroom. Devil's ivy can survive in even dimmer light but thrives in indirect bright light.

Opposite, top left: Bromeliad

Opposite, top right: Boston fern

Opposite, bottom left: This aeonium is an example of a succulent adapting to life in a pot with no drainage. It's not ideal but if you are careful about watering and put pebbles in the bottom, tough plants like this one can cope.

Opposite, bottom right: Kentia palm

I really don't know what led me to make plant-related objects to be honest! Perhaps my daily bush walks (I was taking things pretty easy up in the country) and the little cuttings I'd come home with (mostly everlasting daisies as I love their weird papery quality) led me to make the single stem vessels and I'd found an old bag of my mum's macramé hoard while helping clean out their house.

Where does the humble houseplant fit into your world view?
We both feel most ourselves and at peace when outside. Beach, forest, mountains – they're all equally as great. It feels kind of obvious but surrounding yourself with lots of plants helps to mimic that environment, only with wifi, appliances and 'stuff'. I don't see the plants as stuff. That is the difference, they are kind of like the anti-stuff. They help to filter the air inside your home, sucking in the bad and producing oxygen just like the trees do for us outside.

What impact if any do you think the popularity of houseplants is having in society?
In terms of the popularity I hope people can see the plants as more than an aesthetic trend and that they don't get left out to die if the trend passes. Perhaps people will get to see them as anti-stuff like me, appreciate them for their valuable contribution to their home and then have a think about how important they are in our ecosystem.

Do you have any future plans involving plants and your art?
None in a 3D form. I'm actually feeling the need to paint at the moment and I'm sure plants will be the inspiration behind much of what eventuates. Their shapes, colours, forms and shadows are endlessly inspiring.

How to grow fresh air

Dr B.C. Wolverton

Retired NASA scientist, Dr B.C. Wolverton, was principal researcher for the NASA 'Clean Air Study', a seminal 1980s study into the use of plants to filter air in sealed lunar biospheres. Dr Wolverton continues to research plants, is a consultant to the largest interior plantscape company in Tokyo and is the author of How to Grow Fresh Air *(Penguin Books, 1997) and* Plants: Why You Can't Live Without Them *(Roli Books 2010). Here Dr Wolverton briefly explains his research into the potential for indoor plants to 'grow fresh air'.*

Indoor air is often highly polluted. When we seal our buildings tightly to conserve energy, pollutants are trapped inside. Our modern homes, offices, schools, etc. are filled with synthetic building materials, furnishings and electronic appliances that emit hundreds of volatile organic chemicals (VOCs). Common air pollutants include formaldehyde (found in washing liquids, fabric softener, carpet cleaner and cosmetics), benzene (found in some plastics, fabrics, pesticides and cigarette smoke) and xyelene (found in glues, lacquers, paints, wood stains and printers). Breathing chemical-filled air can cause serious health problems, especially respiratory problems. We spend as much as 90 per cent of our time indoors, so many people now suffer from asthma, allergies and other respiratory problems. We have found that certain houseplants are very adept at filtering these harmful chemicals from the air.

Plants remove indoor air pollutants in two ways. Firstly, leaves absorb certain organic chemicals and destroy them by a process called 'metabolic breakdown'. Secondly, when plants transpire water vapour from their leaves, they pull air down around their roots. Many microbes live on and around a plant's root system in an area called the 'rhizosphere'. These microbes break down chemicals into elements that both the plant and they themselves can use as a source of food and energy. Plants with higher rates of transpiration move the air more rapidly and are better at cleaning air. Plants such as palms, Devil's ivy, Rubber plant and the Peace lily are all excellent air cleaners. Transpiration also increases relative humidity, which contributes to a healthy indoor atmosphere. Generally, plants with more plant leaf surface area will have a higher transpiration rate and more surface area to absorb airborne chemicals. I usually recommend at least two good-sized plants (about 30 to 60 centimetres in height) in a 3 by 4 metre room. A reduction in VOC pollutants of up to 75 per cent can be achieved in rooms where plants are present.

Foliage plants can also reduce airborne microbes in the air provided that the soil is not exposed. Our studies in 1996 showed us that rooms filled with plants have less airborne mould spores than rooms without plants. Mould is a consequence of allowing plant soil to remain damp or having standing water in a plant tray or saucer. To overcome this problem, we recommend covering the soil with a layer of decorative gravel and avoiding overwatering the plant. The layer of gravel quickly dries and so is not conducive to mould growth. An even better option is to grow plants in hydroculture, a soil-free method of growing plants, which eliminates the problem of mould growth. Our studies have shown that plants grown in hydroculture are 30 to 50 per cent more effective in removing VOCs than plants in soil.

For many years, I had a unique hydroponic planter system where the plants in my sunroom were fed only from the waste generated in the bathroom. The waste water flowing through the planter system was cleaned by the plants and microbes, then flowed into an aquarium where we grew goldfish. This system operated successfully for more than seventeen years. I still have many plants in my own home, including Rubber plant, Snake plant, Yucca, Areca palm, Golden pothos, Peace lily and lady palm, and they are all grown in hydroculture. My favourite plant is the Golden pothos, or Devil's ivy (*Scindapsus aureus*). This is one of the most popular plants often

The Rubber plant and Mother-in-law's tongue are top-rated air purifiers.

found in homes and offices. It can be grown in a hanging basket, on trellises, in a standard container and even as a 'living wall'. I am continuing to use this plant in my research. My main focus now is on developing large, built-in systems (such as rooftop greenhouses) where indoor air is piped through a planter system to strip out harmful chemicals before it is released back into the building. Hopefully, one day it will be common for this type of system to be included in new buildings.

Dr Wolverton's top ten houseplants		
Houseplant	**Specialties**	**Formaldehyde** *removal rate* * *(micrograms/hr)*
Lady palm *(Rhapis excelsa)*	Good overall air purifier; removes most air pollutants	876
Rubber plant *(Ficus elastica)*	Emits high oxygen content; removes toxins such as formaldehyde and airborne mould	1171
Corn plant *(Dracaena deremensis)*	Good overall air purifier; removes most air pollutants	1328
English ivy *(Hedera helix)*	Efficient VOC remover, known for removing benzene; removes airborne mould	1120
Devil's ivy *(Epipremnum aureum)*	Particularly adept at removing VOCs; removes formaldehyde, carbon monoxide and airborne mould; increases general indoor air quality	450
Peace lily *(Spathiphyllum wallisii)*	Removes benzene, trichloroethylene, alcohols, acetone and formaldehyde; removes airborne mould	939
Snake plant or Mother-in-law's tongue *(Sansevieria trifasciata)*	Absorbs toxins such as nitrogen oxides and formaldehyde; good plant for the bedroom as it works hard at night converting CO_2 breathed out into O_2	189
Corn plant *(Dracaena fragrans)*	General air purifier; removes formaldehyde	938
Areca palm *(Dypsis lutescens)*	General air purifier; removes airborne mould; good daytime worker	938
Syngonium *(Syngonium podophyllum)*	Very adept at removing CO_2; removes airborne mould	341

* *Removal rate quoted is in a sealed chamber; real-life conditions may vary. Plants are ranked not only on formaldehyde removal rates but also by evaluating their ability to remove a variety of chemical VOCs and indoor pollutants, ease of growth, resistance to insect problems and rate of transpiration.*

A personal jungle

Location
Kyoto, Japan
Residents
Sean Lotman, Ariko Inaoka
and their young son Tennbo
Occupations
Sean: photographer, writer,
manager of guesthouse;
Ariko: photographer, manager
of 500-year-old soba restaurant
business
Place
Home and guesthouse
Plant density
High
Light level
Indirect bright
Plant list
Philodendron (various)
Hoya (various)
Stephania
False aralia

Sean, Ariko and their son Tennbo live in Kyoto, Japan and run a guesthouse from their converted office building residence in the quiet backstreets near downtown. The family lives on the top two floors of the four-storey building and the lower floors are temporary accommodation for visitors. I first encountered their guesthouse when researching places to stay on one of my regular visits to Japan and immediately contacted them to ask them more about the plant-filled residence. The amount and types of plants they have gathered, installed and draped everywhere is a very personal mini jungle built of improvised hanging baskets and containers.

Can you tell me a little about how you met and how you came to be living here in Kyoto?
We met in Tokyo in March, 2005 when I was leaving Japan to return to the US and Ariko had left the US to return to Japan (after living in New York for ten years). We had three weekends together and then didn't see each other again until we met in Nairobi. Together we travelled overland from Kenya to South Africa for three months. The following year we moved in together in Tokyo, relocating to Kyoto in 2011, and moving into our present building in 2012. Both of us work as photographers, though I also write. I run the guesthouse and Ariko runs her family restaurant, which has been in business continuously since 1465. They serve soba and traditional Japanese cakes. We recently had our first child, Tennbo.

Okay so, wow, you have lots of plants here. Who is the plant collector in the house?
While we both did a lot of gardening in Tokyo where we had a balcony, Ariko has been the plant collector in our current household, though I often care for them when she is out. All our plants are in the kitchen/dining room area, which faces south. I would say that her/our plant collecting began in earnest two years ago after moving into our current residence.

Where did you learn about plants?
We never really learnt about plants. Ariko has learnt a bit from her mother and maternal grandmother, both passionate gardeners, and they have given us some advice about caring for them.

Is there any plant here that is really special to you?
We love all of our plants, but the most special plant is probably this enormous what we call the potato vine, about the size of a large bowling ball. It hibernates in the winter and from spring until early fall, sprouts vines that climb the walls and into the rafters of our high-ceilinged dining room.

Which plant here is the longest occupant and can you tell me a little about its history?
We have a plant we received from Ariko's father (who has since passed away) that was our very first. It was sick once and the leaves were coming off. There were little black bugs on the back of the leaves so we had to spray it once a week with a shop-bought pesticide and keep it near air circulation. Taking care of plants in Japan is challenging since winter is so cold and summer is so hot.

How do you find your plants?

There is a plant hunter (that's our nickname for him) in the countryside near Kobe from whom we've bought most of our plants. He is a third generation plant hunter. He travels all over the world, sometimes to very very remote places and buys or collects unique plants he encounters. He has a huge garden/greenhouse in the countryside outside Kobe, sprawling land with thousands of plants from all kinds of climates and continents. It is the most unique place I have ever visited in Japan. We were lucky to have been introduced to him by a friend so we could buy most of the plants wholesale or even discounted.

You are both artists. What part does a home full of plants play in your creative life?

We like having plants and stones, elemental things, natural things in the house. This puts us in a good mood and helps us focus on our work. Definitely collecting more and more plants brings us closer to nature. It's such a warm, beautiful feeling working and relaxing in this space, particularly around twilight or when the sun emerges from the clouds, filling the room with light.

Top: Sean and Ariko call this the 'potato plant'. It is a stephania species – a caudiciform that goes dormant and then sends out new growth each year.

Opposite: Improvised hanging baskets holding a mixture of hoyas and philodendrons. These lend themselves well to hanging gardens as they are both good climbers.

A life's collection

Location
Maribyrnong,
Melbourne, Australia
Resident
Joe Crawford
Occupation
Retired police officer,
hobbyist orchid collector
Place
Greenhouse
Plant density
High
Light level
Indirect bright
Plant list
Slipper orchid
Beech orchid
Pink rock orchid (Pink rock lily)
Rock orchid (Rock lily)
Callus slipper orchid
Cymbidium orchid
Cattleya species

Joe Crawford has been collecting and growing orchids for over fifty years in suburban Melbourne. He keeps the orchids in a series of greenhouses at his home. A member of his local orchid society since the early 1960s, Joe's interest in orchids has been a lifelong hobby. I was introduced to Joe by Mr Kitly's good friend and fellow houseplant fan Karl Scullin. Joe is the dad of one of Karl's oldest friends. The collecting impulse that houseplants engender can be seen throughout the pages of this book and in Joe's orchid collection this tendency reaches its pinnacle. Joe's enduring obsession has resulted in a collection of plants that is testament to what it means to connect deeply with something.

When and how did you begin your orchid collection?
That happened many years ago, back nearly to the 50s. At the time there was an orchid show every year at a large motor car sale showroom in the city. Some of the people in the company were interested in orchids and the management let them clear the cars out and put on a big orchid show for a week each year. I went just to check it out in, I think, 1961 and was most impressed. That was probably in my early to mid-20s so it was over fifty years ago now.

How many orchids do you have here do you think?
Too many! Probably 200–300 would be a fairly conservative guess. I have never even thought about it really. One greenhouse has all my Australian orchids, the other two have all of my Asian and Slipper orchids, and another greenhouse is just miscellaneous types.

Have you ever gone orchid hunting?
No, I haven't. A lot of people know where to go, but it's a fairly closely guarded secret where the native orchid colonies are (in Australia). If the location got out there would be a lot of unscrupulous people who would go and rip them out of the bush and they would be lost. Anyway, it's illegal (to do that). They are very highly protected.

Are the rarer orchids expensive and difficult to procure?
Some people pay up to $1000 for a plant. A lot of them are (legally) imported from America as seeds in flasks, but plants are difficult. Due to quarantine, they are not allowed into Australia. If you get caught you get fined and the plant is confiscated and destroyed so it's pointless doing it. I was in Hong Kong a few years ago and saw a magnificent thing, it was absolutely magnificent, and I wanted to buy it but it was a great big one and I knew I wouldn't get it past quarantine so I just left it.

What is the rarest orchid you have?
I have one that was only discovered in South America about five to six years ago. There was a big stink about it at the time because people went down there and ripped them out of the wild and they got caught and went to jail for about three years. The authorities realised that the best thing to do was to make it available, so they authorised several nurseries to collect the seed to propagate. I got one and had it growing beautifully close to flowering, then all of a sudden it just died. So I got another one. I found someone who had imported a flask of seedlings from America. There were only fifteen or so in the flask and I managed to convince him I needed one. I got it and it's growing here. It's called *Phragmipedium kovachii*.

Opposite: Joe Crawford surrounded by his orchid collection. Photo by Karl Scullin.

Above and opposite: Joe's various greenhouses provide perfect growing conditions, although some of his favourite specimens such as the Rock orchid are tough plants and worth trying to grow indoors.

What is your favourite orchid and why?
I like the Slipper orchid, the *Paphiopedilum*. I've got quite a collection of them. I am just attracted to them. Most of them come from Asia – from China through South-East Asia and even up to the Himalayas. There was a controversy not long ago with those too. They found a new type and people were ripping them out of the wild and selling them. They were ripping these magnificent plants out of their habitat and they were just killing them. The government tried to put a stop to it, but they persisted and so two or three of the collectors were shot. That stopped it.

What is it about orchids that lends them to, at times, obsessive collecting?
The more you find out the more you want to know. Some orchids are not very spectacular as far as flowers are concerned but it's the location they come from and some have got great foliage. The other part is a bit of a competition over who can produce the best results. Some people can grow an orchid and get an extremely good result while others really struggle.

If I don't have a greenhouse, how can I best keep an orchid?
I would hazard a guess that you can't keep an orchid in the house full-time. A lot of people who don't have a heated house bring them inside. They'll have a space where they can put them at night to keep them warm and then in the morning take them out and put them in an airy spot outdoors where they get plenty of good air movement and lots of light. Air movement is the big factor. In nature they grow in high places and you can imagine them growing on the face of a cliff with plenty of air movement. They also need to be where you can give them a really good water then let them dry out, most of them like to dry out before you water them again. Essentially, we need different conditions inside. We need warm, dry conditions to live in. They like to be warm, moist and airy with plenty of wind around them. You don't want to be going to be bed with a gale blowing through the window in winter. If you put them in a spot where they have all their requirements then you might have a chance.

Neighbourly plants

Location
Coburg, Melbourne, Australia
Residents
Jacinta Moore, Amina McPhee,
Poppy (dog) and Coco (cat)
Occupations
Jacinta: photographer, food and
prop stylist; Amina: jeweller
Type
Home
Plant density
High
Light level
Bright to indirect bright
Plant list
Orchid cactus
Agave
Cacti
Cordyline
Canna lily
Rhipsalis
Mother-in-law's tongue
Rubber plant
Boston fern
Pony tail palm
Devil's ivy
Syngonium
Hoya
Aloe vera
Succulents (various)
Zanzibar gem
Donkey's tail
Krantz aloe
Begonia
Freckle face
Chinese evergreen
Elephant ear
Calathea
Nerve plant
Swiss cheese vine
Chinese money plant
Heartleaf philodendron
Haworthia

Opposite: Rubber plant and
Pony tail palm make good
podium specimens.

Jacinta Moore lives in an apartment in a northern Melbourne suburb with her jeweller flatmate Amina, dog Poppy and cat Coco. Jacinta works as a photographer and food and prop stylist and is a regular visitor at Mr Kitly sourcing products for her work. Jacinta's personal photography project of her Orchid cactus houseplant in spectacular bloom sparked a plant-based conversation between us. As soon as Jacinta moved into her ground floor flat she immediately formed a plant-based connection with her Cambodian-born neighbour Deb. This neighbourly connection, along with Jacinta's knowledgeable selection of plant life, makes this an exemplar houseplant story.

Have you always loved plants?
I suppose so, yes. My mother is a devoted gardener, as were both my grandparents, so I've grown up surrounded by plants all my life and probably inherited my love of gardening from them.

Could you tell me a little about your neighbour Deb?
Deb is a very enthusiastic gardener and a collector of plants. She has hundreds scattered around our apartment gardens, as well as inside her home. Deb is Cambodian, but fled to Australia during the Khmer Rouge. She grows many of the plants to remind her of home.

How did you meet?
Deb and I met on the first day I moved in. She gave me a tour of her garden and I reciprocated by bringing her into our apartment to show her the Orchid cactus that just happened to be in full bloom on that day! She promptly showed me her indoor plant collection, and we've been talking plants ever since. She is out in her garden most days, so I will often stop to say a quick hello. Deb can talk for hours about plants and I always come away from our chats loaded with handfuls of gifts – cuttings and seedlings, tropical flowers in cups she folds from banana leaves, or mountains of herbs and vegetables.

I see you have a good example of keeping a hoya cutting in water. Do you find water rooting a fruitful technique?
These are cuttings I took from a giant hoya plant I spotted in bloom a few months ago – the flowers are so amazing, I just had to pinch a piece (or three)! I've just sat them in some water and am waiting for them to set roots before I pot them up properly. I like this method because it's so easy, with the added bonus of getting to see a bit of what's going on with the root system as it develops. I also have a Devil's ivy, a begonia and a rather large piece of Krantz aloe growing in similar set-ups, all having now taken root and waiting patiently for me to work on a more permanent home for them.

Can you tell me a little about the inspiration for the bathroom and the colour theme there. How does it relate to the plants you chose?
Our bathroom is an original 1950s wonder in pink and green – so outrageous – and my favourite room in the house. We quickly agreed to just run with the theme (there is no hiding it, after all) and began hunting, in earnest, for an appropriately co-ordinated plant or two. This quickly opened up a whole new world of plants to me – beautiful pink and green-foliaged Chinese evergreens, the Elephant ear, Calathea, Nerve plants and the Freckle face

Above: An Orchid cactus in bloom. Photo by Jacinta Moore.

Above, right: Freckle face plant and cordyline.

Opposite, top: Jacinta's living room gets quite intense afternoon light so the bottom half of the windows are covered in semi-opaque film which helps protect plants from the burning sun.

Opposite, bottom: Both the Mother-in-law's tongue and Orchid cactus thrive in the afternoon sunlight.

– and all suited perfectly to low light, humid conditions found in bathrooms! The only problem now is lack of space; this room is a definite work in progress.

Can you describe your Orchid cacti collection?
My first Orchid cactus was the product of a late night cutting mission. In a previous house, I used to walk past a giant Orchid cactus hanging over the fence en route to the tram stop each day. I didn't pay it much notice until I saw it in bloom, but from then it was love. I crept out that night to sneak a cutting. The blooms are truly spectacular, but last for not much more than a day. They do very well as houseplants and I have three varieties now – one with a white bloom, one with a red bloom and a Ric-Rac cactus with amazing serrated leaves.

Does it ever get too sunny for your plants?
Yes, I'm forever moving plants around! I quickly learnt that the lounge room windowsill is too hot for most common indoor plants – even one of my cacti had to move, as it just wasn't coping! Our more shade-loving plants have moved to our south-facing dining room. Anything in-between has ended up in my bedroom or the kitchen, which both receive a good amount of light, but without the harsh afternoon sun that hits the lounge room corner.

What is your next dream plant?
We have so many now that I am really making a concerted effort to curb my plant-hoarding tendencies. But I do have a few hard-to-find things on my list that I will make an exception for – *Monstera oblique* (Swiss cheese vine), *Dioscorea elephantipes* (elephant's foot) and a *Pilea peperomioides* (Chinese money plant). I've also been thinking a lot about Chinese evergreens and Heartleaf philodendrons lately, so am trying to imagine where they might fit ... oh dear!

Do any of your plants hold special memories?
Some of my oldest plants have moved around with me for over ten years now, and definitely carry memories of good times past. One with an extra special family connection is a humble little Haworthia succulent, which was given to me as a cutting from my Nanna. She told me that my brother saved up to buy her that plant when he was nine, some time in the early 80s. It's so funny for me to think of my big brother being a sweet little boy before I was born, and I'm glad the story gets to live on in that plant, especially now that my Nanna has passed away.

Plants rule

Location
Brooklyn, New York, US
Residents
Josephine Heilpern,
Sebastian Heilpern
Occupations
Josephine: ceramicist;
Sebastian: musician
Place
Home
Plant density
Medium
Light level
Indirect bright
Plant list
Elephant ear
Mother-in-law's tongue
Devil's ivy
Aloe vera
Succulents (various species)
Madagascar dragon tree
Cacti (various species)
Zanzibar gem
Rubber plant

Opposite: A great collection of
bright-light-loving plants with some
of Josephine's pottery.

Josephine Heilpern is a ceramicist and lives with her musician brother Sebastian in a residential neighbourhood of Brooklyn called Greenpoint. The mid-1900s building sits on a corner. Every room has a window and when the western sun hits, the rooms are showered in sunlight. Josephine's ceramic planters are popular items at Mr Kitly. Her ceramics have decorative detail but she also places a high value on function. This focus comes through clearly in her planter designs because she started making planters for her own plants out of necessity. Josephine's relationship to her plants is the key to how plant function meets ceramic form in her work.

What's the indoor plant scene like in New York?
I remember previously everyone was crazy about cacti and succulents. Now all people want are tropical-looking plants and those mediocre houseplants usually seen in a doctor's office like Spider plants. Maybe it's part of the norm-core fad. In NYC we are very lucky to have an abundance of green public spaces. But apartments are small and decorating can be difficult with limited space. I've been to so many apartments where people don't even have windows! Plants help spaces look healthy and clean. It takes responsibility to look after plants and it's a lot of work sometimes. If I walk into a home with a bunch of healthy plants, I know that person knows how to be responsible (usually).

Have you always loved plants?
Oh my YES! I've always been into plants. My mum always had large plants in the house and I remember petting them and talking to them a lot as a kid. As I got older and moved into my own spaces plants felt important to me, almost adult. I now see myself as a plant collector, it's almost an addiction. If I ever see a plant I don't own I always grab it.

What was your first plant? Do you remember?
I had an Aloe for a really long time and I think it was the very first plant. It got sick a couple years ago, and after trying to treat it I finally had to let it go because it was infecting my other plants. I always have an Aloe around. It's not only a very handsome plant to have and pretty easy to take care of but also very useful. I use it whenever I have sunburn.

What are some of your favourite houseplants?
I have some plants that have been with me for so long, like my largest Jade tree. I have grown attached to it and when it doesn't look happy it worries me. Another favourite is the Elephant ear. It looks so prehistoric to me and I love the patterns on the underside of the leaves. I love the Prayer plant because you can see its leaves folding up and closing at night and that is so fascinating! Whenever I see that it reminds me that these guys are alive. I also love Philodendrons. They are so easy to take care of. If you take some stems and put them in water, they will root and survive. Philodendrons are a great thing to put in vases, much better than flowers because they last forever and when they get too big you can repot them and all of a sudden you have a new plant! I also have a Spider plant that was born from an offshoot of a close friend's plant. Plant propagation is super cool to me. The idea that one plant can link other plants and people is really exciting.

Do you have any special tips on plant care?
My plants get really dusty so I like to stick them under the shower every once in a while. And

all my succulents get a bath. I fill the tub up with cool water and fully submerge the planters in the water while leaving the plant out. Air bubbles start to float up, soaking the soil. When no more air bubbles float up I know that the soil is fully soaked. The plants always look really happy after a bath. I am also a strong believer in talking or singing to them. I am aware of how kooky this sounds but I really do think it helps! My brother is an incredible musician and I think that they respond when he sings to them.

Ceramics is having a bit of a boom time. How have ceramics influenced the way people arrange plants in their homes?
Ceramics are amazing because they have the ability to be both functional and decorative. I think people have been so used to the terracotta planter pots. The shape and colour has been around forever and is very standardised. With the current abundance and popularity of ceramics, the pots we plant in are individualised and can be decorative and functional. I think pots give personality to a plant in the same way ceramic tableware adds to a dish.

What is important to consider when making a ceramic planter?
Drainage is most important. If a planter doesn't have a drainage hole the soil will stay too moist and the roots of the plant can rot, killing the plant. Another thing to think about

is the shape of the planter. Plants grow and sometimes you have to change their homes to allow them to grow more. If the planter has a weird shape it will be hard to take the plant out without disturbing the root system. Plants suffer from trauma and you want to make sure they are always comfortable in order to stay healthy.

What would be your ultimate clay piece involving houseplants?
I really want to learn how to throw giant planters. It's so challenging and takes so much strength and balance.

Do houseplants help the creative process?
Yes! After being in a number of studios I know that the most productive space is a space that is truly your own. It's important to have an aesthetically pleasing space to work in. I'm in my studio more than at home. The plants around me make the space feel alive and breathing. It makes the space feel like it's transforming and moving. These are words and actions we need to be reminded of when we work, otherwise what we make can become stagnant.

Why are plants important to you?
PREAM – Plants Rule Everything Around Me. That's what my brother says. But this is so true! They are the food we eat, the clothes we wear and the air we breathe. Plants are everything.

Above, left: The cacti and Madagascar dragon tree love the bright sunny window.

Above, right: A Zanzibar gem in one of Josephine's planters.

Opposite: A lovely example of an Elephant ear and a great Mother-in-law's tongue in a handmade planter.

The elusive
Pilea peperomioides

Dr Phillip Cribb

Dr Phillip Cribb is a botanist who worked at the Royal Botanic Gardens Kew, Edinburgh as Deputy Keeper of the Herbarium and Curator of the Orchid Herbarium from 1974, until retiring in 2006. Here, Dr Cribb illuminates the botanical treasure hunt of the Pilea peperomioides.

Few plants have puzzled modern-day botanists more than the *Pilea peperomioides*, commonly known as the Chinese money plant. Specimens of it, with its characteristic bright green, fleshy, peltate leaves appeared regularly at the enquiry desks of Kew, Edinburgh and Wisley botanical gardens from the mid-1970s onwards to be returned with non-committal suggestions such as 'Possibly a *Peperomia*', 'Please send flowers next time' or 'We do not identify sterile material'.

Progress on its identification was first made in 1978 when Mrs D. Walport of Northolt sent leaves and an inflorescence of tiny male flowers for identification to Kew. The leaves indeed resembled certain species of *Peperomia*, yet the tiny male flower indicated that it belonged to the stinging nettle family. Eventually, research by a Kew botanist Wessel Marais suggested that the plant was a Chinese species of *Pilea*, named in 1912 by German botanist Friedrich Diels as *Pilea peperomioides*. It had been first collected by George Forrest in 1906 in the Tsangshan Range just west of the ancient city of Dali in western Yunnan province, China.

Over the next few years, further specimens from various parts of the British Isles were sent in for identification. It became apparent that many people were growing this unusual species as a houseplant, passing it on to their friends as cuttings from the readily produced basal shoots, and selling them at church bazaars and fetes and so on. Meanwhile the species was still barely known to scientists who had yet to see female flowers on living material.

The question was how and when did the plant get from the mountains of western Yunnan to Britain. In an attempt to find an answer to this mystery, an illustrated article was published in the *Sunday Telegraph* asking if anyone had any information on the introduction of the plant to Britain. Among the replies received was an essential lead. A family, the Sidebottoms, in St Mawes, Cornwall, had first acquired a plant some twenty years previously. The family had a Norwegian au pair, Modil Wigg, and their young daughter, Jill, then aged nine, went to Jaeren in Norway for a holiday with the Wigg family, who gave the girl a small specimen of the plant to bring back to England.

Following this lead and through further enquiries in Scandinavia, where the plant was equally unknown to botanists, the problem came to the attention of Dr Lars Kers of the Bergius Botanic Garden in Stockholm. He arranged for the plant to be presented on a popular Swedish television program and an avalanche of some 10,000 letters followed, proving the plant's popularity as a houseplant in Sweden. Among these letters was the final link in this extraordinary story. It turned out that a Norwegian missionary, Agnar Espegren, brought the plant to Norway from China in 1946. Forced to leave China in 1944, Espegren and his family were taken by an American plane to Kunming in Yunnan where they stayed about a week awaiting further transport to India. During this brief stay Mr Espegren obtained a live specimen of the plant, which he then brought to Calcutta where he lived with his family for nearly a year. The Espegren family arrived back in Norway in March 1946 with the plant miraculously still alive. Mr Espegren subsequently travelled widely in Norway and often gave basal shoots of the plant to friends. The plant was distributed in this way and is now widespread as a windowsill plant in Norway. From there it was spread to Sweden, England and no doubt elsewhere.

It is extraordinary how this Chinese species, while hardly known to western science, was being cultivated in thousands of private homes in Europe as a result of off-shoots being passed on from one person to another. The piecing together of this Chinese puzzle has demonstrated how effective the combination of amateur gardener and professional botanist can be as sleuth. Part of the charm of the Chinese money plant is the story of its strange and convoluted journey from its home in furthest Yunnan to Northolt and beyond.

Melbourne artist Kirsten Perry is one of the rare people in Australia to own the elusive *Pilea peperomioides*.

The perfectly imperfect

Location
Preston, Melbourne, Australia
Resident
Kirsten Perry
Occupation
Artist
Place
Home
Plant density
Medium
Light level
Indirect bright
Plant list
Chinese money plant
Rhipsalis
Donkey's tail
Fiddle leaf fig
Brake fern
Zanzibar gem
Cast iron plant
Aeonium
Devil's ivy
Fruit salad plant
Palms (various species)
Bird of paradise
Boston fern
Wisteria

Kirsten Perry is an artist who lives and works from her 1970s unit in Melbourne's northern suburbs. Kirsten makes anthropomorphic artworks in jewellery, ceramics and concrete, and also makes animations. She highlights and exaggerates any mistakes in her hand-built objects and through humour aims to challenge the idea of perfection in both art and life. Plants often play a central role in her creations and she has created many planters and plant-inspired objects for Mr Kitly. Kirsten is also the only person I know of to possess the coveted houseplant Pilea peperomioides *in Australia. She discovered it among the stalls selling indoor plants at her local trash and treasure market. Kirsten's humour and warm regard for the wonkiness and imperfections of life are played out in planters that are individual and highly appealing.*

How would you describe your place?
It's a small, humble 1970s unit that is a nice space to place some artwork and plants. I converted my garage into a studio where I can make a mess. My lounge ends up being a transitional storage space for my artwork. I hope the style reflects my personality, maybe a bit quirky and unusual but also hopefully warm and inviting.

How did you begin making planters?
I started playing with clay in my jewellery and then wanted to make larger objects. Most likely I wanted a few pots for myself, then I applied for my first solo exhibition back in 2011. Some of my initial concepts were tracksuit planters. I saw the plants as sculptural elements that added to my work.

Do you have plants in mind when you make your planters?
Sometimes I have a vague idea of a particular plant when I start but mostly it comes once I have made the planter. Sometimes it takes about two to three repottings before I am happy with the relationship. Usually there is no rhyme or reason as it's like matching two different personalities.

Do you have planters that you are particularly fond of?
My soccer ball planter with the Zanzibar gem from Mr Kitly takes pride of place in my bedroom. I love the terracotta accents showing through the uneven white glaze on the slumped form teamed with the shiny leafed fronds. I also love some of my new text-based agate-ware planters. Their matt, unglazed texture goes well with green shiny leaves. The text is based on comments from good friends, so they have another level of emotional connection for me.

Would you call yourself an avid indoor gardener?
Avid, not sure, but enthusiastic definitely! I still tend to kill some, which means maybe I still have a way to go. But the idea of an indoor jungle sounds wild. I see some pictures of people's living space online and marvel at the greenery. Something to aspire to. My Mum's green thumb has influenced me a lot.

Is there anywhere in your house where plants really thrive?
By my lounge/kitchen window is a lovely sunny spot, especially in winter. My Fiddle leaf fig loves it there. I'm working on what plants best suit my bathroom as it's a little darker.

Above: Kirsten's soccer ball planter shows off a gorgeous Zanzibar gem. Artwork by Anna White, David Neale, Brendan Huntley and Kirsten complete the bedroom tableau.

Opposite: The *Pilea peperomioides* in Kirsten's bathroom in a line-up of her handmade planters.

Is there a plant you really want that you don't have?
I'd love a big Fruit salad plant, big palms, a Bird of paradise, a few more hanging plants and a bushy Fishbone fern.

What kind of plants do you like to keep indoors?
Anything low maintenance that does not require much water is great. I love my Fiddle leaf fig and hanging Devil's ivy. A variation in size, shapes, colour and texture is best, sort of like building a composition. You can sit back and make adjustments and additions, like an artwork in progress. I also like taking cuttings from my Mum and friends as it is a reminder of the connection we have.

Do you have any good tips on keeping plants happy?
Dust them so they can breathe more easily and emit loving vibes when you do this. Surely they will respond well.

Can you tell me how you found your Pilea peperomioides?
It was from a local trash and treasure market where the one dollar entry fee is extremely good value. I go for the Nonna plant stalls. I have a vague recollection of finding my pilea plant there. Amongst the red geraniums, chilli bushes, Yuccas and succulents, I'm sure it lay hidden. Recently I returned with a photo, on a mission to find the person I had purchased it from. Easy, I thought. I asked three stallholders and the response generally followed the line of:

Me: Hi I was just wondering if you sell this plant?
Nonna: Oh, yes, I have but not here. But look, look I have other lovely plants. Half the price of what you pay in the shops.
Me: Oh really? Do you have anymore?
Nonna: One at home but small. How about this plant, it's beautiful. Only $5.
Me: Oh, ok. Can you bring it next week?

Nonna: No, it's not ready. How about this plant? It's beautiful. It grows well inside. $5

Me: Ok, sure, I'll get it.

Hmmm. They were either telling fibs or being very evasive about sharing their pilea. I guess I just got lucky one day.

Have you found it easy to take care of?
Thank goodness, it more or less takes care of itself but maybe the admiring vibes I send it add to its happiness. I think if it was difficult to take care of, my stress would have killed it by now. I did notice once I replanted it into a bigger pot, it thrived. I'm eagerly awaiting another off-shoot baby so I can start sharing the joy around.

Do you think plants make a good creative muse?
For sure, I'm always thinking of building happy homes (planters) for them. Also looking at them makes me happy and more tranquil which improves my creativity. In my studio I have a vine from the neighbours' wisteria that has crept through the window and grows along the wall. I think it likes it there and it makes me smile when I think about its stealth-like sneakiness.

Do you have any future plans for artworks including plants?
I like the idea of always including plants in my work. Perhaps people will recognise them as a sculptural medium. More plants make people happy, I say.

The beauty of plants

Location
Tokyo, Japan
Resident
MA
Occupation
Plant planner
and producer
Place
Various shops
Plant density
High
Light level
Various
Plant list
Wax plant
Begonia
Vanda orchid
Tillandisa (various)
Narrow-leaved palm lily
Fockea
Ruffled fan palm
Philodendron imbe
Xanthorrhoea species
Dicksonia species

MA lives and works in Tokyo and has been working with plants for fifteen years. His job title, plant planner/producer, refers to his work of the last eight years as a plant buyer and supplier to plant stores throughout Tokyo. I met MA while on a business trip to Tokyo and he showed me around some of the plant shops and galleries he works with. He has strong ideas regarding the way plants are bought and sold and valued, and it is refreshing to hear considered opinions put so forthrightly. In his spare time MA takes photo portraits of plants. His photos are full of admiration for plants in all their varied glory. His careful selection of plants for shops paired with his personal plant photography make his dedication to plants clear.

Can you tell me about your job?
My job is to find the beauty of each plant and then supply to retail stores. I have been working in this plant supply company for eight years and working with plants for fifteen years.

Where do you find your plants and what makes you decide to buy a plant?
For work I directly buy from farmers. For myself I buy from plant shops or different specialist shops or from roadside shops I discover when travelling. If a plant is beautiful or if I see potential in a plant I buy it.

The term 'plant hunter' is sometimes used in Japan and abroad to describe people who actively seek out rare and unusual plants. Would you say you are a plant hunter?
I am not a plant hunter because plant hunters are explorers who travel and seek out plants that no one knows of. I do not go into the jungle to collect my plants. I go to the markets or purchase from importers, so I collect plants that are available in the market. What is important to me is how I can discover the character of each plant and be able to show this in its best light. Whether a plant is unique or rare is not so important to me.

Did you study horticulture?
I did not study at school. While working in a flower and plant shop, I learnt from both books and experience. In books or at school there is usually one answer and this doesn't apply to all problems.

Why do you take plant portraits?
Each plant has its own beauty so I take an image that best shows this. I zoom into the plants many times because I want you to see its beauty first rather than the type or species of plant.

Your job seems unique to Japan. I cannot imagine anyone having this type of 'plant producer' job in Australia.
There are other people like myself who search out plants and sell on to other people. This may not be common but there are two wholesale nurseries in Australia that export plants (*Xanthorrhoea* and *Dicksonia*) to Japan who do similar work to me. There are also many collectors of orchids and succulents in Japan. With different plants there are different techniques necessary, so each collector selects a specific type of plant. These groups meet

Opposite: MA trims a narrow-leaved Palm lily at Time and Style, Tokyo.

up regularly and exchange information. These types of collectors have existed since the Edo period (1603–1868).

Can you tell me a little about the history of plant collecting in Japan?
In Japan there has always been a culture of enjoying plants. Japanese people have always enjoyed looking at the details of things. Historically people would have collected plants during their trips to the mountains. During early times there was no heating so Japanese people enjoyed growing native plants such as ferns and variegated plants. Then foreign rainforest/indoor plants began to be imported for the Tokugawa clan (samurai who were running the country 1603–1867). These were not available to everyone. Other Japanese people were still only collecting native plants. Then during the Meiji period (1868–1912) more nobility began collecting plants and more foreign plant importing began.

In Japan there are some innovative botanical artists who do plant-based art such as Azuma Makoto whose recent artwork involved launching plants into outer space. What is more important – to be an artist or to be a gardener? Or should one be both?
I think if you have a strong concept and are able to communicate with an audience that is a great thing. But when something is just cool or unusual/unique, this is not long term and a waste of design. For me the most enjoyable thing about plants is the time you spend caring and communicating. I am afraid that plants might become a short-term interest (a fad) and therefore disposable. To understand the enjoyment of plants it takes time. If plants fall into the up and down cycle of trends, this enjoyment will never be understood. In my job and in my private work I follow the same philosophy that everyone will find their own honest way of enjoying plants. Plants should not be difficult, they should be open to everyone. Once there is this dialogue, there will be a greater understanding of art and design.

Can you tell me about your philosophy relating to the buying and selling of plants?
Each plant has a different meaning and a reason for its existence. Plants all play different roles and we enjoy them in different ways. When buying and selling we need to think of the balance and harmony of the plant world otherwise our appreciation will be lost. Lately the industry is more focused on the buying and selling instead of the plants themselves. They are only placing value on rare and uniquely shaped plants. Plants cannot be manufactured. It is difficult to grow plants with today's society of quick consumerism. With regards to distribution, it's necessary that buyers support and protect the farmers' work by giving advice about quantity and types of plants needed. With regard to retail, plant shops shouldn't just sell plants to customers who are new to plants. As plants are living creatures, each is different and cannot be cared for from an instruction manual. It is important to first discuss the way of enjoying plants instead of focusing on a particular plant. This opens up different worlds. This applies to many things – a narrow view will limit your enjoyment.

Do you have many houseplants in your home?
I live in an apartment. I used to experiment and see if the plants would grow, so I had many plants. At one point I had so many that I couldn't live freely in my house. Now I have moved them to a greenhouse at my business. At home I have about ten planters of various shapes and sizes, and sometimes I experiment with these.

Opposite: Vanda orchids with a healthy root display hanging at FUGA, Tokyo.

p. 74, clockwise from top left: kalanchoe, photo by MA; philodendron imbe at Time and Style, Tokyo; Wax plant at Buzz nursery, Tokyo; Ruffled fan palm at Time and Style, Tokyo.

p. 75, clockwise from top left: Fockea at Buzz nursery, Tokyo; pine cutting; anthurium, photo by MA; shop assistant at FUGA, Tokyo.

Plant
window

Opposite: Phil's window predominantly
consists of many different species of
hoya and rhipsalis.

Phil Huynh lives in a converted mattress factory in the inner city suburb of Collingwood. His large, plant-filled window was the entrance to a walkway that connected his building to the building across the narrow street. Phil is a florist and often visits Mr Kitly in search of ceramic vases for his work. He is a difficult man to track down with a busy schedule splitting time between city floristry jobs and foliage foraging on farms. The link running through all Phil's work is his considered and artful approach to nature and sustainability. His window garden is testament to this and has become the stuff of legend.

How do people react to your plant window when they come in?
It's usually just a wow. I think a lot of people think that I've 'decorated' it. But it hasn't been like that – it's just a natural progression. When I first moved in there was only a couple of plants here, then I started adding more and amassed this collection.

It looks like you've got a really diverse range of plants but the number of species is actually quite limited. It is pretty much just rhipsalis, hoya and succulents, all quite tough plants. In terms of plant species, have you chosen only ones that can care for themselves a little bit?
I think the thing is when you are not often at home you have to look for plants that will adapt to these living conditions. So here it's mostly succulents and hoyas, which are fine as long as they get enough light.

How has your connection to plants come about?
My grandfather was a rice farmer in Vietnam and when we moved over here he worked as a landscaper. So I grew up working in the garden with him. On weekends I would follow him and we'd do people's vegetable gardens and we'd do our own garden. He taught me everything about what to do in the garden and composting. Then when I was studying in

Boston I went to visit my friend Tara who had an organic flower farm in Silver Lake in LA. I loved working on her farm so anytime I had a break I would fly over there and help her out. I grew up working with flowers and just being on farms with greenery.

There is a difference between indoor plants and the cut flower. A plant is something you are trying to keep alive for as long as you can but cut flowers by definition die once cut. What are your thoughts on sustainability in your work as a florist?
I mostly forage the flowers and foliage I use from farms. Farmers are happy for me to do this because it's a type of pruning in most cases. I have also gone to nurseries and bought plants to cut and to use in floristy though. I think that comes from wanting diversity. The cut flower market is very narrow in what they supply, especially for the kind of arrangements I want to be doing. I hardly ever go to the flower market. The flower market is a 5 am start. It's a concrete shed and all the flowers are lined up with a lot of the foliage the same height – it's not inspiring for the kind of work that we do which is kind of loose and wild.

There is a plant (I believe a type of variegated Pelargonium or geranium) planted into a beaker on your table that's a lovely manifestation of the idea of

beauty in decay. I can see it also has zero drainage as well so it's fighting against all the elements.
Yes, it really shouldn't be growing in here at all but I love it and it's quite prolific. If you cut the dead stems off it will grow more but I just can't, I refuse to cut them off. I should probably give it a little bit of compost or fertiliser as well. No drainage is easy for me – it's very hard to find good pots with plates. I really like the look of beakers though. You can see the roots growing through and that's what I love the most, seeing all that.

Which plant was the very start of the collection?
The curly hoya. If you look at the other side it's yellow because it's in harsh light but this side is green. But it's healthy because it flowers. All my hoyas flower. It flowered twice this year and once last year. They must like really harsh light because the light in here is quite intense. Sometimes I think it's rather cruel to have all these plants in here in the harsh light but if I just water them constantly then they're fine.

You have a nice Elephant ear.
I love Elephant ears. They just need to be constantly moist.

You have a Fiddle leaf fig. What do you think about the current boom in its popularity?
It's amazing how the demand for them has just shot through the roof but no one knows how to look after them. I had a client come to me and show me photos of hers and it's amazing! All this beautiful top growth. She asked 'How do I stop it from growing?' I said what is happening here is what everyone wants! She said she just wanted a little one and I told her if she wanted it to stay small to put it in a dark room otherwise it is hard to find the perfect spot for them and you've found it. They can start dropping leaves within a week of being moved, and they don't like under or over-watering, or direct light.

How would you describe your interior style?
Funnily enough this is not my personal style at all. I love clean lines and white space. My ideal space is very minimalist. You would have no idea looking at all this stuff everywhere but I am so minimal, almost that really stark designer look. I would love to have a really big marble bench and a big battery vase of just foliage, and that would be the only crazy element. That's my ideal. But I also love living in here as well. Everything here has a story.

Right: The rhipsalis and hoya here enjoy bright light and have relatively low watering needs.

Opposite, bottom left: A beautiful pelargonium species, which Phil said is called a Brocade leaf geranium. In most cases pelargoniums go dormant in winter and so should be underwatered then.

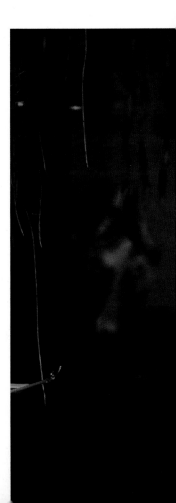

The Butterland bathroom

Location
Newstead, Victoria, Australia
Residents
Katie Marx, Greg Hatton,
and their young children
Hazel and Minnie
Occupations
Katie: florist; Greg: furniture
maker, landscaper, stonemason
Plant density
Medium
Light level
Indirect bright
Plant list
Creeping fig
Bird's nest fern
Baby's tears
Begonia
Rope Hoya
Rhipsalis
Maidenhair fern
Hosta
Fiddle leaf fig
Lily of the valley
Nasturtium
Staghorn fern

Katie Marx and Greg Hatton and their two young daughters live in a 100-year-old butter factory in a regional Victorian hamlet called Newstead. Katie is a florist and Greg is a furniture maker, landscaper and stonemason. My first visit to Butterland was when I commissioned Greg to make some salvaged-wood cutting boards for Mr Kitly. Buttterland is a sprawling space that includes multiple living spaces, Greg's large furniture workshop and areas left deliberately unoccupied, including the old foyer and a high-ceilinged main room and mezzanine. Katie and Greg have renovated their home to retain its industrial heritage with the beautiful patina of age. The bathroom has a particular connection to the building's history as it was the lab where butterfat was tested. Butterland is an evocative and quite majestic space, and the bathroom is the green jewel in its crown. It's the classic houseplant interior decor idea of a potted fern in the bathroom taken to the next level by florist Katie's natural affinity for greenery.

What is the history of Butterland in a nutshell?
We purchased the property in 2010 and it has been a labour of love ever since. Newstead had a thriving dairy industry and the butter factory operated until 1976, producing prize-winning butter. After this it became a candle-making factory for twenty-five years so there were inches of wax over every surface, including the 7-metre-high ceilings. The place was a mess having had no maintenance or repairs for a very long time.

How has moving into Butterland changed your life?
It's changed in many ways. We feel more settled here and love being in the country. Our lives are still very busy, with two daughters and Butterland evolving into our working space. We are still making furniture and doing flower installations, which we love, but hosting events as well.

What did the Butterland bathroom look like when you first moved in and did you have to do much fixing up?
The bathroom was actually the original lab used to test the butterfat for the factory. It already had the solid concrete benches and draining floor so it lent itself to being a wet room. We installed the big green bath and connected the shower and filled it with loads of plants. Its great because you can and do get water all over the floor and it just drains away so kids love it. You just have to remember not to leave your clothes on the floor.

Bathrooms are such a classic place for houseplants to thrive, why is this do you think?
Humidity and light. I think it's a closer environment to outside than say your kitchen or bedroom.

Can you tell me about the Creeping fig on the bathroom walls?
We love vines so the idea is it can go as crazy as it likes over the walls and ceiling and if one day it dies, the skeleton will be left and another vine will grow. It is planted in an old air vent used when the bathroom was part of the original lab for the butter factory. It's a fairly large 'pot' but I do fertilise when I remember and water a couple of times a week. It's never been pruned as I want it to go nuts.

Opposite: The Butterland bathroom in all its glory. The window faces south, but the overhead skylight provides ample light for plants.

How long has it taken to get to this coverage?
It was planted about two years ago so I'm estimating in five more years the bathroom ceiling will be green.

How much light does it get?
The bathroom gets a lot of light because of the glass opening skylight but never direct sun as it is south facing.

How does it cling to the walls?
It has small tentacle things that stick very firmly to the walls.

Do you use houseplants in any way in your floristry practice?
Yes, definitely, all kinds of plants get used in my work. I quite often have their roots exposed or cut their amazing leaves for bridal work.

As a botanical artist, a florist, could you talk a little about your thoughts on nature and plants?
I have a huge respect for Mother Nature and consider her to be the greatest artist. I often feel totally awe struck by the patterns on bark or the intricacy of veins in a leaf, even the combinations of colours and patterns together.

What is your approach to houseplant care?
If it's not too hard to look after then it's got a chance, and don't over-water.

Where or how have you learnt everything you know about houseplants?
There's been a lot of trial and error. Some have flourished in the bathroom while others haven't liked it at all. I have killed three Fiddle leaf figs and I can never get a string of pearls plant to live more than six months. Some things that totally flourish are Begonia rex, Bird's nest ferns, Baby's tears and hoyas.

Do you have a favourite plant here?
Baby's tears – I love it. It reminds me of being a kid and making fairy gardens. It's so delicate and soft.

What would be your ultimate installation involving houseplants?
An old overgrown glasshouse with plants going crazy everywhere. To set a table laden with nasturtium seedlings, hand-blown glass and fragrant Lily of the valley amongst this foliage would be so beautiful.

Above: The Creeping fig is slowly taking over the bathroom wall and ceiling. It was planted in an air vent and needs the good light from the skylight to thrive.

Opposite, top: Katie found this Staghorn fern on the side of the road and nursed it back to health by 'feeding' it banana skins. Bananas are a good source of potassium and other minerals for plants (and humans). Katie tucked whole banana skins in between the mounting board and the basal fronds of the fern.

Opposite, bottom: Baby's tears and Bird's nest fern love the humidity of the bathroom.

Arranging
with plants

Location
CBD, Melbourne, Australia
Residents
Madeline Kidd and
Masato Takasaka
Occupations
Madeline: artist,
drawing teacher;
Masato: artist,
sushi chef, teacher
Place
Home
Plant density
Medium
Light level
Bright indirect
Plant list
Fiddle leaf fig
Peace lily
Bamboo palm
Parlour palm
Orchid
Hoya

Madeline Kidd and Masato Takasaka live in a modern apartment on the third floor of a converted warehouse apartment block down a narrow laneway in the Melbourne CBD. Life is fast in this area full of bars and restaurants and their apartment is a quiet light-filled oasis above the hustle and bustle. Madeline is an artist and drawing teacher and Masato is an artist, sushi chef and teacher. Madeline is the plant collector of the household. I have known Madeline and Masato for many years and they are active participants in Melbourne's contemporary art scene. In her art practice, Madeline explores decor and the domestic space by using popular symbols of interior decoration such as paintings, abstract sculptures, fruit plates and of course plants, in installations of domestic scenes. This practice makes Madeline a most interesting person to talk to about the idea of plants as decor and her own connection to plants.

What led you to an interest in houseplants?
I've always been into furniture, art and all things decorative. I have a have a bit of a fetish for 1960s *Home Beautiful* magazines too. Houseplants are an obvious interest within that sphere.

Your Fiddle leaf fig is a superb specimen. How long have you had it, and how much has it grown in that time?
A friend I'd describe as a proper gardener suggested that I purchase this about five years ago. It fitted into a hatchback then, so it's roughly doubled in size in that time.

How do you keep it so healthy?
I have to admit I just add water. I do however, dust the leaves occasionally and do some spritzing every now and then.

What elements do you think are necessary to maintain happy and healthy plants inside?
Watching over them. Sensing any discomfort. I have a large Peace lily plant that collapses entirely when it doesn't get enough water. It's actually very helpful as the rest of them all tend to suffer in silence.

Are there any drawbacks to keeping plants in an inner-city apartment?
Repotting plants can be difficult. It's something architects and planners should give more thought to. There should be soil chutes on all balconies in the city. How else are we supposed to keep cool in these hot boxes?

What piece of plant care advice have you found to be most useful?
If it ain't broke don't fix it. Watch which way the wind is blowing.

Do you think there are any plant myths that need to be busted?
Houseplant obsessives might come across as caring, kind, loving, naturalists, but deep down I suspect many of us are calculating, obsessive perfectionists. It's a great hobby.

Where or how have you learnt what you know about houseplants?
The little that I do know I have picked up through a process of trial and error and by asking people who work in nurseries lots of inane questions whenever I get the chance.

Opposite: A regular mist spray, leaf clean and good light provide great conditions for Madeline's very happy Fiddle leaf fig. Once it finds a spot it likes a good tip is not to move it.

Above, left: A Bamboo palm is a
nice sentry in the apartment foyer.

Above, right: Artworks by Madeline,
part of her 'Painted Gardens' show.

Opposite, top right: A Peace lily
in a wooden planter is a classic
houseplant choice and one of the
all-time toughest survivors of low
light and neglect.

*Every piece in your home seems very carefully
curated. Do you have a particular aesthetic
approach to choosing new plants for your home?*
Well, yes, I suppose I do. I look at size and
shape, texture and colour, and then read the
label on the plant to see if it would work in the
location I have in mind.

*Could you talk a little about how plants and plant
themes make their way into your paintings and
sculptures?*
Plants appear in my work as decorative
flourishes here and there, and as a way of
adding colour – greenness – and texture to
a painting or sculpture. Sometimes they are
the central subject of a work. I've done a lot
of paintings of flowers, for example, or trees
within landscapes.

*What role do you think houseplants play in the
creation of a domestic scene?*
In the CBD, oxygen is important or at least the
feeling of greenness or freshness. Encouraging
bird life and insects is also key. A very noisy
cricket showed up a couple of months ago. I
was enjoying listening to it until I realised it had
eaten all my mint.

*Can you give a personal example of the role plants
play in interior decor?*
I think, historically, plants were often a signifier
of class and taste, in a similar way to cut flowers.
For example, my grandfather was an architect
and had very specific tastes. A cloisonné pot
containing yellow orchids in the lounge room; a
perfectly trained hoya vine on the balcony. He
designed the house as well, and the plants were
an extension of the built environment, They
were part of the overall design just as the yellow
rose print on the sofa was or the single velvet
curtain in the entrance area.

*Would you ever use an actual pot plant in a gallery
installation?*
I used real houseplants in an installation I did a
few years ago at the Melbourne Cricket Ground.
I transformed the changing rooms where the
footballers shower and bathe into a romanesque
bathhouse with rose petals and greenery. I
thought the environment could do with being
feminised somewhat, which is perhaps the
understatement of the year. The project went
ahead due to some kind of corporate policy
where the MCG were trying to interact with
different sections of society that don't usually

engage with sport. I don't think there were any
sportspeople at the opening but the public
seemed to be genuinely entertained by the
exhibition. I can remember lots of people wanted
to get in the bath to experience it more fully. More
recently, I designed the interior of a new boutique
gym in Hobart, Artgym. Plants were very much
part of that concept – again, combined with
artworks – and the overall concept of a tranquil
oasis in the middle of the city. It's also a nod to the
idea of 'clean green' living, in that the gym uses
natural sound cleaning products, and I felt that
the plants would add to the feeling of freshness
and vitality in the space.

*If you could only choose one plant for your house,
what would it be?*
I would probably go for size and choose the
Fiddle leaf fig. It has an undeniable presence.
It's most likely going to have to be permanently
here as I have no idea how it would fit in the
elevator. Any attempt at lopping it would be a
tragedy of epic proportions; I would hear the
silent screams.

Hanging out with plants

Opposite: The Iko Iko plant line-up includes a Fruit salad plant, Fiddle leaf fig, croton, palms and a plant they know as the 'Coin tree', potentially a relative of the Chinese money plant.

Iko Iko is a studio, showroom and shop on the top floor of an 100-year-old building in downtown Los Angeles. It occupies an entire floor, with huge skylights and windows around the perimeter of the east and north walls bringing in bright natural light. The space is shared by Kristin Dickson-Okuda who makes clothing under the label Rowena Sartin, her partner Shin Okuda who makes furniture under the name waka waka, and Kimberly and Nancy Wu who make leather bags under the name Building Block. I first met Kristin and Shin when I was writing a blog about Japan called ii-ne-kore and we began to follow each other's creative pursuits from afar. With Iko Iko, Kristin and Shin investigate new models of the process of making and presentation that centre on experiencing the unexpected. The shop and gallery spaces they create as part of this ongoing investigation have invariably included plant life.

Your gallery and store space creates a context for what you make. How important are plants as part of that?
Plants give a space life, literally. They provide beautiful texture and one that requires attention and care. We take a casual, non-hierarchy approach to plant types and containers. It's more about a casual attitude, how we can all exist together. Come hang out, plants.

You have said that your store model centres on change. Could you elaborate a little on that?
The store space is changing as our work changes, so we allow the space to reflect that in a modular sense. The furniture is all by Shin, so we don't have built-in shelves, racks or tables. We want the store to be re-installed with each new idea. We decided to just focus on what we ourselves produce so that the space reflects the spirit of our work, or more so that there is a conversation between the environment and the work.

How would you describe the LA houseplant scene, if one exists?
I think many people gravitate towards cacti and succulents because the climate is so accommodating. In LA it also depends on where you live. I have friends who are more houseplant people and some that are more desert plant personalities. Sun and shade folks.

What was your first ever houseplant? Do you remember?
A Maidenhair fern that I came close to killing every week. I've learnt from it.

Do you have plants in your home as well as here in your work and shop space?
We have a Gingko plant at home, but mostly our green life is from flowers picked on neighbourhood walks. I like to have small arrangements according to what I find on a walk or a smell I want inside.

What are your favourite go-to houseplants?
I like anything that mimics a wild hairdo.

Would you call yourself a green thumb?
I think I can manage, but I'm no expert. I go on instinct.

Above (L-R): Chinese evergreen, Pony tail palm, croton, Fiddle leaf fig.

Opposite, clockwise from top left: Palm species; calathea; Umbrella plant, cycad.

Where or how have you learnt everything you know about houseplants?
Through my very green-thumbed friend Hope. She lives in Oregon and at one point her entire living room was filled with plants like a commercial nursery. The plants were like her extended family members, all living under one roof.

What's the best piece of advice on houseplants you have received?
Take on what you have time to care for. This is very important for me. All the plants at the store are a substantial caretaking, so I try to be particular with what we incorporate into our home life.

Are there any artists or movements that, for you, have a strong and inspiring connection to plant life?
I prefer flower experiments for the home sphere. I love ikebana, the Sogetsu school, in particular. The Japanese approach to seasonal tendencies is a good way to live for me.

You have a mighty healthy Fiddle leaf fig in your space. What are your tips on keeping it healthy?
I got that from the nursery across the street

from our old location. It's survived well and in the same container with just one repotting. I water everything, treating the leaves like skin. When it's dry, they get more water visits. I think the Fiddle leaf fig just comes from a really good gene pool. I can't take that much credit.

How do houseplants figure in your creative process?
I like a casual, everyday relationship to plants and flowers. It's interesting to figure out the containers and placement for them and how that creates a conversation in a room. A plant is a living organism, so it deserves proper placement in a space.

What do you like about plants?
Each plant has its own personality. Each one grows in its own way, some rely more on you than others.

What would be your ultimate installation or artwork involving houseplants?
I would love to find the smallest houseplant in existence and have it placed in the middle of a gigantic, white-walled room with a light that rotated like the sun's path in a day.

Design for plants

John Patrick

John Patrick is a landscape architect, TV presenter and author. Here he describes a classic mid-20th century, self-watering design for indoor plants.

The self-watering planter designed by the esteemed Australian industrial designer Richard Carlson for Melbourne homewares company Décor took an idea widely used in Scandinavia and simplified it for the domestic market. The pioneering Australian design was first released in 1987 and was one of many high-profile designs developed during the 1980–2000s by Richard Carlson, whose BYO wine bottle carrier is a permanent exhibit in the New York Museum of Modern Art (MoMA).

Richard Carlson prepared the elegant and refined designs for Décor corporation while I was asked to test their efficacy for plant growth. Brian Davis at Décor was a perfectionist who employed the very best people in his design work. I designed a garden for Brian in the Melbourne suburb of Brighton in 1980 and he was my first Australian client after moving to Australia from England.

The system uses the soil within the planter as a wick, drawing water into the potting mix at a rate that reflects the plant's use and evaporation as a result of the room's atmosphere. All the home gardener had to do was top up the water well as needed and occasionally add a soluble fertiliser to keep plants fed. The system was straightforward and simple and very effective.

Well-known interior designer Tony Wolfenden provided advice about the original colour range that suited Carlson's elegant and timeless forms. He wanted to use colours that fitted into the family home without becoming the focus, and that allowed the beauty of the plants to speak for themselves. The pots are as beautiful and appropriate a design today as they were at the time of their release, and clear evidence that simple, clean designs of this quality have lasting appeal.

Opposite: Almost thirty years after their initial release, Mr Kitly collaborated with Décor on a new range of sizes and colours of this classic self-watering planter. Planter by Mr Kitly with Décor, art direction and photography by Tin & Ed.

A natural influence

Location
Brooklyn, New York,
United States
Resident
Shino Takeda
Occupation
Ceramicist
Place
House
Plant density
Medium
Light level
Indirect bright
Plant list
Philodendron selloum
Devil's ivy
Rhipsalis
Hoya
Heartleaf philodendron
Mother-in-law's tongue
Succulents
Chinese evergreen

Shino Takeda is a ceramicist living in an apartment in Brooklyn, New York. Shino was one of the first artists I asked to be part of Mr Kitly. Shino's graduated use of colour in her glazes evokes scenes of nature and her approach to glaze has been highly influential on many of her contemporaries. She has also been part of a small ceramic studio planter-making boom of recent years, producing various planters for Mr Kitly. Shino's plant-filled main living area is soaked in light, and her apartment provides an additional indication of her deep connection to nature that is so evident in her ceramics.

Can you describe your apartment?
I live in a new condominium building. The space is square, loft style. Windows face south – pretty much the whole wall is windows! The apartment was like a greenhouse, getting sunlight all day long. Now there's a new tall building next to it, so not so much light.

Could you also describe your ceramic practice?
I hand build all my ceramics. I see beauty in perfect imperfection. I am influenced by nature around me. Colours are my most important voice.

You have a really amazing art collection. Do you ever think of plants in terms of art – arranging them like paintings?
Plants got first pick of space, and wherever left was filled with paintings and sculptures! (And the areas that I don't want my cat to walk around are filled with plants.)

What are your favourite go-to houseplants?
They change all the time. I am into cactus now. I love having different ones next to each other. Some are wild and some are calm. So many different kinds – like New York!

Do you have a particular plant here that is extra special to you?
I have this huge tropical plant, and I don't even know its name [Philodendron selloum]. It came from my mother-in-law's high school. This plant was almost dead, but then it got happier and happier in this apartment! So it is very special for me.

You have some plants growing in water I see. What plants do you find are best for that?
Ivy plants. I trim plants once a while, but then I feel bad throwing these cuttings away, so I put them in water. But then they grow roots! So more plants for me. I have too many plants now. I give some to my friends once they grow roots.

What's the best piece of advice on houseplants you have received?
Giving too much water is worst than not giving them water.

What is your process when you sit down to make a ceramic planter?
I don't think much about plants when I make a shape. But when I glaze, I imagine where I want to see the plant – desert, ocean, forest, with sunset or sunrise.

What is your favourite clay piece involving houseplants?
I made a black vase called 'Tobe!- Fly!' It's a bowling ball shape. It's a black ball with three holes to put flowers or cuttings, and it has two wings.

Why are plants important to you?
Having greens around me is healthy and healing.

Opposite: Shino's casually artful plant collection includes a Mother-in-law's tongue, rhipsalis, hoya and a Devil's ivy.

Bottom, right: Devil's ivy and
heartleaf philodendron are great
choices for rooting in water.

Opposite, top: A huge Philodendron
selloum rescued by Shino is now
thriving. It is a low demand plant
that responds well to some love.

That 70s feeling

Location
Balaclava, Melbourne, Australia
Residents
Meredith Turnbull,
Ross Coulter and baby Roma
Occupations
Visual artists
Place
Home
Plant density
Medium
Light level
Bright indirect
Plant list
Umbrella plant
Cocos palm
Madagascar dragon tree
Rhipsalis
Chain of hearts
Hoya
Arrowhead plant
False aralia
Hare's foot fern
Bromeliad
Aeonium
Fruit salad plant
Devil's ivy
Donkey's tail
Prayer plant
Heartleaf philodendron
Rubber plant
Maidenhair fern

Opposite: A Fruit salad plant, a Donkey's tail and a Prayer plant complement Meredith's arrangement of artworks including pieces by Minna Gilligan, Steven Rendall and Milly Cobb.

Meredith Turnbull is a visual artist, writer and curator. She lives with her partner Ross and daughter Roma in a strikingly spacious apartment in an old suburb of Melbourne. The original layout and fixtures of the 1969 apartment give a feeling of light and space that is unusual and a good aesthetic match for plant life. The main living areas and patio face east, and the bright morning light is perfect for Meredith's plant collection. When I became aware of her research interest in craft, decor and her personal interest in 1970s houseplant books, I was curious about her thoughts on art and craft and how they relate to houseplants.

What led you to a love of plants?
My mother Jenny inspired my love of plants. She is an avid gardener and when I was little she would section off parts of the garden for me to have as my own. I have an early memory of her coming to my school. She taught our class how to make tiny little terrariums in ice cream tubs and other containers.

Are you and Ross both plant lovers or does one have more of a plant connection?
Ross enjoys the plants too but I bring them home and look after them. I'm always asking, 'Do you think there is room for one more?' or saying something like 'The laundry could do with a plant'.

Do you think your apartment style has influenced your plant collection?
Definitely. Although we had some of these plants in our old apartment in the city most of them are new, and we tend towards a sort of 1970s feel that's in keeping with the apartment. We try to go for things that appeal to our aesthetic sensibilities and not always things that are in fashion, like a choosing a Weeping fig over a Fiddle leaf.

You have a great collection of books on plants. Do you collect houseplant books mostly for information or for aesthetic inspiration?
Most of my books are from op shops and these are collected for their aesthetic appeal but their gardening advice is really spot on too. I have lots of books on indoor plants and a few on landscaping. Some of my favourites are the *Reader's Digest Practical Guide to Home Landscaping* (my copy is from 1973) and *The Small Garden book* by John Brookes (1977). A lovely recent purchase was George Seddon's *Your Indoor Garden in Australia* (1978). The book collection gives me lots of ideas for our indoor plants but also for our little garden.

What plants are good choices as survivors for indoors do you think?
Something with a strong leaf structure and density like the *Monstera deliciosa* or Heartleaf philodendron or a Rubber plant. Devil's ivy is also one of the best indoor plants that I have come across. It's beautiful as a trailing specimen or you can grow it in a standing form and trim it regularly. We also have a beautiful Madagascar dragon tree that someone left by a rubbish bin. A lot of its tips were damaged but we repotted it and put it in the kitchen where it gets afternoon sun. It has grown back beautifully and seems very happy now.

The Umbrella plant – what a specimen! Can you tell me about it and your tips on keeping it happy?
The Umbrella plant is a favourite because I've had it for such a long time. I've pruned it quite severely in the past and repotted it a few times, and it just keeps growing and growing. When we moved from the city we had quite an alarming attrition of plants one winter while we were away overseas. The Umbrella plant was one that survived. So I'm attached to it for this reason. I've had to clean the leaves a few times very thoroughly to keep it happy and healthy and treat scale. It likes a regular water, not a soak, and having its leaves cleaned.

How do you make decisions about arranging your plants?
Mostly I try and select a spot in the house where I think the plant will do well, depending on the light and temperature. I try and follow the care instructions and read up on what they like. I prefer things that are low maintenance, and they tend to stay in the same spot in the house for long periods of time, especially if something is thriving. I always go for green and interesting structure over flowers or bright things, and we do tend towards cane and timber baskets and plant stands for most of our plants.

Do you feel like your indoor gardening is another creative pursuit?
Looking at and after plants is very relaxing and being in a space with plants just feels right to me. But also researching indoor plants is so closely related to my research into interiors. Plants are living things but they also function as objects in space. Sometimes this type of thinking happens simultaneously. Looking at plant books is a sort of down time for me but it can also stimulate new ideas for artworks, particularly structures, sculptures or ensemble works that I want to make.

Do you think houseplants have historically had quite a close relation to craft or folk art practices (for example, the relationship between macramé and plants, the terrariums of the 1970s and studio potters making planters)?
The relationship goes deeper and predates the 1970s craft movement. Our love of houseplants is still so closely related to the creation of hothouses and glasshouses and the care of plant varietals and specimens in collections indoors, not only for ornamental but also educational benefit. The 20th century craft movements also have a particular legacy that includes the role of craft and its relationship to its environment and to nature from earlier times. For example, William Morris and the Arts and Crafts Movement and Ebenezer Howard and his ideas around the Garden City Movement in the UK from the 19th century. We see this relationship in architecture too, in Frank Lloyd Wright's organic architecture like the Prairie School houses or Fallingwater (built in the 1930s). In simplified terms what these different examples share is a sense of nature and the lived environment as aspects or factors to be brought together into harmonious existence with one another for the purpose of health, education and pleasure, as part of a pursuit of a good life, for the mind, the body and the soul.

Opposite, top left: Artwork by Meredith in the window, an installation from 'Melbourne Now' exhibition, 2014.

Opposite, top right: A fine example of an Umbrella plant.

Opposite, bottom: Plants on the kitchen bench include syngonium, False aralia and Hare's foot fern. Artwork by Dane Lovett.

Above: Artwork includes pieces by
Rozalind Drummond, Lisa Radford,
Katherine Huang, Ross Coulter,
Rene Cosgrave, Minna Gilligan,
Steven Randall and Milly Cobb.

Bottom, right: A Devil's ivy totem
is one of the most versatile and
forgiving plants.

Opposite: Artwork by Michael
Ciavarella and a Devil's ivy make a
perfect corner.

p. 108 (L-R): Cocos palm, Madagascar
dragon tree, Chain of hearts, rhipsalis
and Maidenhair fern all beautifully
co-existing. The Maidenhair fern is
well-positioned to be more protected
from the sun than the light-loving
rhipsalis hanging directly in front of
the window.

Plant trades

Location
CBD, Melbourne, Australia
Residents
Stanislava Pinchuk
(visitor Evie Cahir)
Occupation
Stanislava: artist;
Evie: illustrator
Place
Stanislava's studio
Plant density
Medium
Light level
Bright direct
Plant list
Devil's ivy
Pot belly fig
Succulents
Fruit salad plant
Philodendron selloum
Fiddle leaf fig

Stanislava Pinchuk is an artist who works under the name Miso. Her recent artworks are highly detailed pinprick 'maps' on paper. Alongside her professional artwork, Miso has an ongoing personal project of doing homemade tattoos. I visited Miso's Melbourne studio to talk about her art, tattoos and plant trades. I was interested in the way trading tattoos might reference the trading of cuttings and plant advice, and the way that both can engender community. During our conversation Stanislava mentioned her friend Evie's drawings of plants and cuttings and showed me some images of her work.

Evie studied illustration and works in Melbourne as a freelance illustrator. She describes her work as being 'about mostly sunsets, small steps taken throughout the day and, of course, plants'. Seeing Evie's drawings of plants inspired an immediate connection to the botanical drawings of indoor plants found in Victorian-era herbarium collections and, more recently, with the indoor plant books of the 1970s and 80s. Evie's renditions of houseplants are a contemporary take on this long tradition. So of course I had to include Evie in this story as well.

Stanislava, you have an ongoing project of homemade tattoos, which are only completed for trades. You trade tattoos for things such as dinner, drawings, a rock, a photograph and plants. What began this idea and where is it taking you?
Stanislava: Yes! Tattooing is a really intimate thing for me, and since I'm only tattooing friends outside of my studio hours, it feels really strange to put a monetary value on that. So I really love the idea of trading, of alternative economies.

Have you done many houseplant trades?
Stanislava: Yes loads of houseplants came from it, including one in my studio that came from a friend who works in a nursery. No one had any idea what it was, or where it came from. I'm trying to keep it alive, figuring out bit by bit what it needs. So funny things like that, which wouldn't have been there if money were a part of it!

Do you also do a lot of trades?
Evie: Yes! For me, trading has always been a great part of creating and sharing work. I remember as a kid 'trading' drawings with Mum for other things I wanted! The trading of artwork for objects, meals, plants and potential friendship should be a legitimate form of currency.

Have you both been known to also share plant clippings with neighbours or friends?
Evie: I have always been the recipient of clippings, mostly from my friends. I'm still learning how to be a responsible plant owner.
Stanislava: A lot of my plants are from cuttings, and my ivies have multiplied a lot of siblings.

Evie, your self-published book, SOIL, is about growth and obsession. Can you talk a little more about the ideas behind the project?

Opposite: Fruit salad plant on a Mr Kitly 'Triangle Leg' plant stand.

Evie: The houseplants, ferns and cacti painted for *SOIL* are created in order to transform a routine experience such as watering plants, watching the small growth and changes, and the sunlight and shadows created. Along with being obsessed with trying to capture the light and texture of the plants, I want to create a body of work that promotes an active immersion in and awareness of small but beautiful moments.

Are there any artists who you think are looking at houseplant culture in an interesting way?
Evie: Artists such as Ebony Eden and Sarah McNeil, and photographers such as Brian W Ferry and Jacinta Moore are all documenting and capturing houseplant culture in beautiful and inspiring ways.
Stanislava: Japanese architect Ryue Nishizawa's Tokyo Garden House bowls me over every time I see it. I just think it's the perfect way of living with plants. That line between public and private space, filtered through the plant life that Tokyo has always had in this really

incredible, next level way. Sou Fujimoto does it really well too. I also really love Makoto Azuma. He's from another planet!

What is the best advice on houseplant care you have ever received?
Evie: The best advice on houseplant care was to stick to hardy succulents – leave the Maidenhair alone.
Stanislava: I didn't know about making garlic spray to kill aphids for a long time! That was really welcome advice.

Do you have a favourite houseplant?
Evie: The collection of houseplants in our bathroom. The cuttings, little ferns and succulents in there make going to the toilet poetic.
Stanislava: I've been growing two Fiddle leaf fig trees in my apartment for years. It's not always easy to grow them in Melbourne, but they're getting so tall now! I love seeing them grow, especially over the winter.

High density living with plants

Nigel Bertram

Nigel Bertram is a Director of NMBW Architecture Studio, and Practice Professor of Architecture at Monash University, Melbourne. Here Nigel discusses the contribution potted plants can make to the quality of life lived closely together.

The idea of plants integrated with architecture has a lot of currency, and for good reasons. Plants make us feel cooler, provide shade, soften buildings, are highly decorative and make people feel better. On a larger scale and en masse they can also make cities function better. Items such as 'green walls', 'green roofs' and community gardens are in hot demand and often used as selling points for new apartment buildings or whole urban redevelopments. Unfortunately they also often fail, or plans are abandoned before even starting. Plants exist in a fundamental tension with the desires of architecture to be structurally stable and keep water out. Prohibitive costs, technical difficulties, planning regulations and constraints associated with body corporate management conspire to undermine the best intentions.

In stark contrast to all of this sits the Beverley Hills apartment complex in South Yarra, designed by architect and developer Howard Lawson and built in 1935–36. While other apartment dwellers are struggling to get any plants to grow at all, this property of forty-two dwellings closely packed into two six-storey buildings is alive with vegetation at every scale. Plants overflow both in the gardens outdoors and the inside communal areas. An enormous Moreton Bay fig tree dominates the rear of the block, a dense grove of palms protects the communal swimming pool, geraniums and climbers cascade out of private balconies and potted plants of all sizes and varieties are everywhere. There are plants in pots on balustrades, in stairwells, in front of doorways, on ledges, on old chairs and side tables in corners, in large urns on staircases and used as bollards to manage vehicles. Plants are stuffed into windowsills and herbs grow on ledges and in small spaces beside paths. There are succulents, natives, flowering plants and tropical species – exotic, decorative, whimsical and formal specimens. The effect is completely eclectic. The multitude of potted plants and more conventionally grounded garden combine together to form a landscape with a truly charming personality. There is no one singular character but the combined expression of many contributors and individual tastes, cumulatively developed and added to over time with a relaxed mixture of the carefully designed and the ad-hoc. Some plants were established by the directors of the apartments' managing company, others self-seeded, some provided by current owners and tenants, and many left behind by ex-residents.

The current director of the apartments' managing company, Don Bennetts, is 77 years old and has been a Beverley Hills resident for forty years. His wife Christine is a keen gardener and unofficial custodian of the collective landscape. They believe that the culture that has developed at Beverley Hills is the result of decades of engagement and passion on the part of its residents. For Don, it all starts with Lawson's architecture. The high level of detail, idiosyncrasy and decoration provokes a response in residents. Lawson integrated planter boxes into windowsills and balustrades and each apartment was provided with its own window box for growing herbs. Now a culture has developed where residents regularly swap cuttings and look after each other's plants when they go away.

The plants in pots at Beverley Hills range from the monumental to the disposable. Despite differences in style, species and soil type, the greenery and life all these different plants share merges together from a distance to make a soft layer of privacy and variety: a type of decorative veil around the architecture. Urban landscaping on this micro-scale gives pleasure to the immediate owner but also makes a contribution to the whole that can be perceived and enjoyed by others. There is an intimacy gained by adding private plants to small indoor and outdoor spaces that can also increase the cumulative perception of greenery apprehended from eye level

within a dense urban environment. Small spaces such as courtyards, stairs, porches, verandahs and balconies all have an important urban role to play and their planting and personalisation can affect the quality of the public realm.

Potted plants could be placed in the category of 'loose furniture'. Their location and arrangement is provisional – there always exists the possibility of another way. Perhaps this impermanence helps people to go along with the decisions of others and wait to see the results. Residents are able to engage actively and creatively in shared areas of the property without the need for body corporate consensus.

Beverley Hills is unique, but there are lessons to be learnt that could be followed in new buildings as we build more apartments and live at higher densities. Apartment buildings are types of collective houses, which entail a degree of shared ownership and collective expression. But for such an identity to develop authentically, an allowance for customisation and modifications by residents over time is required. We need less total design as pre-packaged solution and more design intelligence encouraging the action and involvement of individuals. We need more tolerance of 'messiness' and allowance for change. This all requires us to think of high-density living more as a process than a product – as we do of the city itself.

Planting is a form of self-expression and an easy way to create better, more peaceful small urban spaces. The example of Beverly Hills has shown that potted plants and other impermanent, furniture-based customisations are low-risk, low-cost and high impact ways of allowing a culture of diversity and personalised expression to evolve within the centrally managed and often sterile environments of apartment living. Designing the spaces and structures through which such interventions are allowed to flourish can help us to live better, as we live closer together.

A plant enthusiast

Shabd Simon-Alexander is a textile artist who lives and works in Brooklyn, New York. She shares an expansive loft space in an old factory building with artist friend Antoine Catala. I first became acquainted with Shabd's textile design work when researching for my design blog, ii-ne-kore, and having heard rumours of her amazing plant-filled loft, she was one of the first I invited to be in this book. It is a pleasure to share a little of Shabd's enthusiasm and deeply felt connection to her plants.

What inspired you to start collecting plants and how did you end up with so many?
When we first moved into our loft I wasn't used to having so much space and light – NYC apartments are famously small and dark. Rather than fill our home with furniture and objects I thought I would build an indoor veggie garden. When I realised indirect light wouldn't work for that, it became an indoor jungle. We moved in with a few plants and have amassed the rest slowly over the years. A lot are gifts or hand-me-downs and I love how each of these is a representation of a friend, family member or moment in life. Most of the big ones were adopted from people moving out of the city or out of big lofts. We adopted four large trees and a bunch of little guys from the octogenarian feminist artist Hanna Eshel when she moved out of her amazing West Village loft into a retirement home. Most of the small ones I pick up at local shops. Antoine says I'm like a crazy cat-lady, but with plants. I think it's the best hoarding you can do. I'd rather have beautiful plants cleaning my air than buy a bunch of clothes or other stuff to fill my house with.

How do people react when they visit your home?
People are always amazed at how full of greenery our loft is. Kids have the best time because they really can get lost inside the jungle.

Would you say you had a green thumb?
I used to think I had a black thumb until I moved into our sunny loft. I've realised over the years

that half of caring for plants is finding the right fit for your lifestyle and your space. I've learnt I can't care for anything that needs a lot or a little water – ferns and succulents are hard for me.

How do you manage plant maintenance with so many plants to look after?
We don't have a routine for our plants, but if you love your plants and enjoy spending time with them you can just tell when they're thirsty. Antoine takes care of the big plants and I take care of the small ones. (He's big, I'm small.) He typically waters the big ones with the leftover water from washing our salad greens, so they get watered regularly enough without too much effort. Small plants need water more often and I have one or two that are canaries in the coal mine and warn me when all the little ones are thirsty.

What are your top houseplant choices? Can you choose any favourites?
If you're new to houseplants, ivies and spiderwort are forgiving and rewarding. They're typically lush and grow fast. Alternately, it's amazing to have something bold and dramatic like one giant palm or a tree of some sort.

Do you have a particular plant here that is extra special to you?
I have different relationships with each of my plants. There were a couple of adoptees that were really hard to get to thrive, but are doing so well now that it just warms my heart. There's Elmer, who I adopted already named.

Opposite: Plants relish the indirect bright light of Shabd's loft apartment.

An indoor garden

Location
Ivanhoe, Melbourne, Australia
Resident
Mary Featherston
Occupation
Interior designer
Place
Home
Plant density
High
Light
Indirect bright
Plant list
Fruit salad plant
Calathea
Maidenhair fern
Wax plant
Bird's nest fern
Creeping moss
Taro plant

The work and life of Mary and Grant Featherston forms an integral part of Australian design history. For thirty years their design practice produced work across many fields of design. Mary specialised in the design of children's learning environments and Grant in furniture design, and it was a work and life partnership that lasted until Grant's death in 1995. The Featherston's close relationship with influential modernist architect Robin Boyd resulted in the extraordinary Featherston House, designed in 1967. It became one of Boyd's most acclaimed houses and has been Mary's home for over forty years. I first visited the house as part of a Robin Boyd Open House series and fell for the lush indoor garden. Many years later I was able to visit again and ask Mary what is it like to live with a garden in her living room.

I have read that part of your brief to Robin Boyd was for a house based around 'living in a courtyard'. Why was that idea important to you both?
Our brief was for a 'shed-like' building incorporating a garden. Robin's own house in South Yarra [now home to the Robin Boyd Foundation] is built around a courtyard and one could enjoy this open green space from all living areas in the house. We also wanted adaptable, interlinked spaces that would accommodate a wide variety of domestic and professional settings.

Boyd took the brief a step further and made a garden actually inside the house. How did that come about and what did you think of that?
Robin, who was a friend and colleague, understood our deep appreciation for nature and natural forms. His design makes nature an essential element – through views to the 'bush' block and the indoor garden and pool. This is an endless, and continuously changing, source of visual and aural beauty.

The garden is planted alongside carpet and furnishings. Is it difficult to maintain a garden indoors?
Prior to building the house we sought expert advice – to be told that the idea was unworkable. Plants like cool damp conditions and people need warm and dry environments. We have experimented over the years trialling various plants. Many did not survive for various reasons – lack of birds, rain to remove insects etc. The current limited palette of plants thrives with very little maintenance but does require regular fine water spray.

What is the most pleasurable element of the indoor garden?
Magical moments ... mid-summer when late-afternoon sunlight bounces off the surface of the pond and projects huge rippling reflections on the brick walls and sunlight illuminates the brightly coloured fish swimming against the dark green background of the pool.

Has the house, and in particular living with (albeit contained) nature so close to hand, had any influence on your own design practice?
My current design/research practice concerns design of learning environments for children in schools. I believe it is essential for children – and their teachers – to have connections to nature through their surroundings, through observation, study and research, and in the fabric of the building.

Opposite: The Featherston House has a completely internal garden with a series of platforms floating over the greenery and pond.

p. 128, bottom left: Creeping moss and ferns thrive around the moist pond area.

p. 128, bottom right: Creeping moss climbs alongside the entry stair.

p. 129: The Wax plant is an Australian native and vigorous twining climber. It can be difficult to coax hoya to flower indoors, but here it does and fills the space with its wonderful perfume.

Robin Boyd and his garden rooms

Tony Lee

Tony Lee is the Director of The Robin Boyd Foundation. Founded in 2005 the Foundation continues the work and spirit of Robin Boyd through public learning programs aimed at deepening the understanding of the benefits of design. Here Tony introduces Robin's approach to design and discusses the role of courtyard gardens in Boyd's work.

Robin Boyd (1919–1971) is possibly Australia's most well-known and influential architect. He worked predominantly in Melbourne between 1938 and 1971, designing over 280 projects. The majority of these projects were residential – bespoke houses, project houses and multi-unit developments. Trained as an architect, Boyd also worked as an author, journalist, public commentator, filmmaker and academic. He held a passionate belief that design could enrich people's lives, and the common thread through all his work was a dedication to communicating the benefits of good design to the general community.

Philosophically Boyd was a modernist, so he believed that good design began with a limited material palette, simple forms – often experimenting with and making visible a building's structure – and passionately rejecting all applied decoration and featurism. But unlike many of his contemporaries who adhered to a rigid approach to design based principally on function, technology and aesthetics, Robin Boyd was a humanist by nature and possessed an intuitive ability to reflect his clients' personalities and embody their aspirations in the design of their buildings. For Boyd, good design recognised the emotional power of buildings and spaces and how they could affect and influence people, contribute to their wellbeing and, most importantly, 'touch their heart'.

During the 1950s and 60s when Boyd was in practice, it was widely believed that technology would ultimately address all human needs and that fossil fuels were unlimited. There was very little awareness of the environmental and social sustainability matters we face today. Boyd pre-empted these concerns and embraced a very sensitive approach to existing landform, planting, natural light, sun, prevailing views and our climate when designing buildings.

Whether designing domestic, commercial or institutional buildings, Boyd recognised that the Australian ideal of being 'outdoors people' is compromised by our erratic climate – especially in Victoria – so he included protected outdoor spaces in most of his buildings. Often these spaces were semi-enclosed or fully enclosed courtyards that became sheltered garden rooms protected from harsh winds and weather. These courtyards were always planted to provide shade, and soothe and delight the eye, and often included herbs and fruit trees.

In a letter sent to his clients Zelman and Anna Cowen, Boyd describes the central courtyard that forms the entry to the house he designed for them in 1957. 'I picture the central courtyard here not as a usable space but as a small, cool, high, lushly planted focal point. You enter through it and all rooms except the bedrooms feast on it. The roof of it I picture as a woven, open slat affair raised five or six feet above the main roof to allow through ventilation while still shading the rooms from summer sun.'

A courtyard garden in the centre of Boyd's Zoology Building at ANU in Canberra provides light to laboratories and a delightful place for staff to lunch. Courtyards and indoor gardens at the entry to houses and offices ensure a calm transition from public streets to private indoor spaces. In the house he designed for his own family at Walsh Street in South Yarra, Victoria, the central courtyard and garden is the largest 'room' in the house. At the Featherston House in Ivanhoe, Victoria, the courtyard actually becomes the house; the garden is completely internal. Platforms without walls, appear to hover in the internal 'landscape' replacing traditional rooms.

Opposite, top: Drawing by Robin Boyd of the Cowen House, 1957, courtesy Robin Boyd Foundation.

Opposite, bottom: Cowen House, circa early 1960s. Photograph Mark Strizic 1928-2012, © The Estate of the artist.

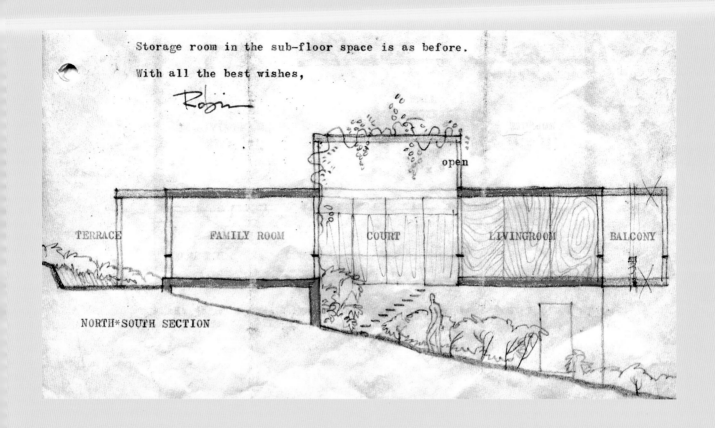

Storage room in the sub-floor space is as before.

With all the best wishes,

Robin

TERRACE   FAMILY ROOM   COURT   LIVINGROOM   BALCONY

open

NORTH*SOUTH SECTION

What are your ideas for keeping healthy indoor plants?
Many people want to grow indoor plants but they can't keep them alive for more than a year because those indoor plants are naturally for outdoors and are difficult to grow indoors. Plants indoors are difficult because of, firstly, lack of sunlight, secondly, temperature control and thirdly, moisture and water control. If we solve these problems, indoor plants will become more popular. We need to make the maintenance easier. This is what I am thinking. Lack of sunlight: sell plants with indoor plant lights as a set. Temperature control: indoor plants (rainforest plants) will not grow below 15 °C. Below 10 °C they will lose their leaves, so the temperature needs to be above 15 °C. Moisture and water control: it is common knowledge to give water when the soil is dry. This is the only advice we can give customers.

To solve this we need an indicator to show the timing of when to water plants or, instead of planting with soil, encourage people to use hydroponics, which is an easier way of watering plants.

What is your plant retail philosophy?
I am not interested in just selling plants but helping customers maintain their plants. Many people think that plants are short-term disposable products but they are living things. This is what I want to communicate.

What are your favourite indoor plants?
I don't have particular favourite plants but I like plants that are always moving upwards. All plants grow towards sunlight. I feel the power of life from this natural growth.

Green on white

Location
CBD, Melbourne, Australia
Resident
Anny Apostolidis
Occupation
Jeweller
Place
Studio
Plant density
High
Light level
Bright direct
Plant list
Boston fern
Devil's ivy
Philodendron selloum
Maidenhair fern
Rubber plant (variegated)
Ficus alii
Bird of paradise
Kentia palm
Chain of hearts
Bromeliad
Fruit salad plant
Song of India
Fiddle leaf fig

Opposite: Anny's light-filled studio is home to an array of well-looked after plants including a Bird of paradise, Philodendron selloum, Rubber plant, Maidenhair fern and Boston fern.

Anny Apostolidis makes jewellery under the name Mavro Jewellery and works from her light and bright studio in the Nicholas Building. She uses natural semi-precious and precious gems and gold and silver in her work, the beautiful natural resources available to a jeweller. I learnt about Anny's work and studio when she bought some Mr Kitly plant stands and posted online a beautiful picture of them in her studio. Anny's studio is a classic example of how well plants can work in a clean white space, and how creating that kind of clean and green space can be a great starting point for making beautiful work.

Can you describe the light in your studio?
It's lovely and bright. My windows are north-facing so I get continuous light throughout the day. I rarely need to turn the lights on. It's the perfect light to work in.

How do people react when they come into your space?
Walking around the hallways of the Nicholas Building is quite dark. There's not a lot of direct light around so when you open my door it's this bright, white lush jungle. People are always amazed and the first things they comment on are the plants and the windows.

Can you tell me a little about your houseplant journey. Have you always been a big houseplant fan?
I've always loved houseplants but I think it was when I had my own studio that my love for them really flourished. They're like my little pets and I love watching them grow.

Have your houseplant choices or affiliations changed over time?
Definitely. I've really learnt what plants work best in my kind of space and what plants don't. I used to always want a big Fiddle leaf fig but now I prefer more lush plants like ferns and my beautiful Philodendron.

Is there any plant here that is really special to you?
I suppose my Maidenhair fern, because not only have I managed to keep her alive but she's growing really well! I love Maidenhairs but they're so temperamental. It has become my mission to have a healthy, happy, flourishing one. I'm very proud of this specimen.

What is the best tip on houseplant care that you have ever received?
I get great tips from everyone all the time, especially about the Maidenhair. I've combined all those care tips into one routine and it seems to be working – water every day with a full glass of water, keep it sitting in water (not too much though) and mist its leaves every few days.

Why do you have plants in your studio?
Firstly, they make the space what it is, but they are also great air purifiers. I try not to use a lot of chemicals but it's unavoidable when making jewellery sometimes. Having the plants makes me feel like maybe I'm not inhaling as many fumes as I would be otherwise.

Which plant here is the longest occupant and can you tell a little about its history?
The biggest Devil's ivy was a gift from my friend Stanislava, who has a studio in the building too. She and I trade things all the time. In this case I gave her a ring and she gave me this plant. She's the one who told me about plants being great air purifiers. I get a lot of plant tips off her.

Above, left: This Fruit salad plant's aerial roots are a sign of a happy and healthy plant.

Above, right: Peaches and Keen's globe terrariums are made from recycled beer kegs.

Opposite left: A Peace lily in a neon orange pot makes for a striking combination.

Why do houseplants feature so strongly in your work?
From the very beginning our work focused around plants, and we put this down to both living in small apartments without proper gardens. It was our way of feeling connected to nature, and something that we continue to explore in our work. The lushness of green plants seems to complement our use of colour and vice versa. Plants have a beautiful way of finishing our creations so it made sense to also use them as a starting point for our artworks.

Your first exhibition featured an oversized hanging globe terrarium. It was such a unique take on a well-referenced plant craft. Can you describe the making of those?
The globe terrariums were really exciting to make at the time. Terrariums hadn't yet

become mainstream and we were offered some eco beer kegs by the lovely lady who runs our local cellars. With our skinny arms we were able to plant them up using the guidance of a book on terrariums we'd found at the op shop. Despite the resulting scratched arms, we were so thrilled with the result. They all sold at the exhibition, but I kept this one as it got a dent when we were setting up the exhibition. I'm not sure how much longer it will last though as Scout seems to think it's a ball for him to bash against the wall.

What are your thoughts on the modern-day terrarium comeback?
So many of these old crafts from the 1970s such as weaving, macramé and hanging planters have had a massive revival in recent years. We like

the concept of taking an old idea and putting a contemporary spin on it. People making their own is great. It's so much more satisfying to create something than buy it in a shop.

Why does the idea of the hanging garden resonate so strongly with you?
We began exploring ways to hang plants pretty much as soon as we started working together when Lucy made some crocheted hanging planters. From there it evolved to woven beaded hanging planters. New and creative ways to incorporate plants into our work progressed from our desire to incorporate plants into our homes in new and creative ways. The desired outcome is always one where the plant becomes an artwork in itself. There is so much possibility in hanging

gardens. The central themes in our work are plants and colour, and by using these as the main concept we have been able to evolve and develop new hanging ideas based around these common themes. There are so many interesting plants out there – the inspiration is endless.

What would be your ultimate installation or artwork involving houseplants?
A project that would take us around the world to explore amazing plants and use them in new artworks.

A giant in a glasshouse

Bree Claffey

Right in the centre of Melbourne's Royal Botanic Gardens there is a densely packed houseplant heaven called the Tropical Glasshouse. Built at a time when the interest in collecting tropical and rare foliage plants was at a peak in the early 1900s, its functional brick and glass appearance belies the treasures held within.

The tropical glasshouse is pure inspiration for any houseplant enthusiast. This engrossing collection includes twining philodendrons, giant Elephant ears, drooping ferns, winding hoyas, Birds of paradise, zebra-striped bromeliads and hot pink cordylines. There are also rare plants such as the Black pepper tree or the Coffee plant that make you immediately want to go home and try to grow them yourself.

Here you will witness ordinary houseplants free to reach their weird and wonderful best. A Heartleaf philodendron twines relentlessly around roof rafters and cascades down walls, hinting at a takeover. And an Elephant ear reaches giant proportions with grandly arching stems and huge shield-like leaves.

The glasshouse also houses an example of the rock star of the botanical world, the Titan arum. This is a relative of one of our most well known houseplants, the Philodendron. But when the Titan arum flowering event occurs it tends to overshadow all others in its genus.

The plant is the progeny of a seed given to Sydney's Royal Botanic Gardens by Sir David Attenborough, who travelled to Sumatra and brought back seeds for conservatories around the world. The Titan arum's common name 'Corpse flower' was given by Sir David during the filming of his BBC *Private Life of Plants* series. The name was given because of the pungent rotting meat stench given out by the plant's flower at the start of the growth cycle. The particular stink attracts the flower's pollinators.

The main reason for its rock star status is its remarkable flower (or more accurately, inflorescence). It is the largest of its type in the plant world, reaching over 2 metres tall at its peak. It can take up to seven years to build up to flowering but once it starts, it's preposterously fast and grows at a rate of 18 centimetres per day. The flower first opens at night and gets so hot from growing so quickly that it steams. It steams!

It's quite stunningly massive but seen up close it's not just the sheer size that's striking. The texture and colours are remarkable. It has a yellowy, velvety 'phallus' with an almost decadent purplish fringe around the base. It is difficult not to anthropomorphise. You can feel like you are in a scene from the *Little Shop of Horrors* confronting a benign version of Audrey II as you gaze at the surreal massive yellow infloresence.

The flower lasts at its plump peak for just three days then begins to slowly crumple, bend over, shrivel and dry up – a process quite beautiful to observe. It returns back to a dormant tuber to save up its energies for its next flowering event. The flowering is rare and unpredictable. A plant might flower every year for three years, or it might not flower once over a period of fifteen years.

I can't help wondering what the Tropical Glasshouse's plant curators make of this big rush to see the Titan arum in flower. The flowering event gets so much publicity and is so popular it necessitates an extensive queue management system of ropes set up on the lawn in front of the little glasshouse. When people come through most rush straight past the front area where the full and glorious collection of plants is and make straight for the Titan arum, not stopping to look at so much as a flower or variegated leaf on the way through. They miss the best part – all the good houseplants are there in the front.

Opposite: The Titan arum in flower at the Tropical Glasshouse in Royal Botanic Gardens Melbourne. Photo by Jacinta Moore.

A case of natural history

Location
Tokyo, Japan
Residents
Daisuke Tsumanuma and
Kenichi Yamada
Occupations
Product designers
Place
Home and studio
Plant density
Medium
Light level
Indirect bright
Plant list
Staghorn fern
Airplant
Lipstick cactus
Council tree
Pachypodium
English ivy
Cactus (various)
Xerographica

Daisuke Tsumanuma lives in a suburb about half an hour by train from the centre of Tokyo. His small apartment is also the studio of the design project 10^{12} TERRA where he works with Kenichi Yamada. After studying together at university, Daisuke pursued a career as a game engineer and Kenichi as a web designer. But their love for creating products and a shared interest in natural history drew them back together to create 10^{12} TERRA. I have stocked their work at Mr Kitly for many years. Their handcrafted products tell of the enduring artisan traditions of Japan and of a new generation of makers creating original products that are a reflection of a unique perspective. Coming from a background of computers to now work with the organic world of plants, 10^{12} TERRA redefines terrarium as a new type of specimen-case based on the designers' interest in natural history.

The 10^{12} TERRA hydro vessels are a cross between a vase and a terrarium. What was the design idea and process behind them?
We have always been interested in root systems and the growth of a plant. We both loved collecting specimens and studying natural history in our spare time. We wanted to create a product that would show the entire plant, like a specimen – the growth of the plant as well as the growth of the root system. We were surprised to discover that cacti could be grown hydroponically. We thought that would be our original idea for TERRA's product. The name comes from the number of cells produced per day by a human body (10^{12} = 1 Tera) and the word 'terrarium', and symbolises growth and life. We chose these words as we wanted to create products that represent life's growth and new discoveries.

Is hydroculture relatively new in Japan or does it have a long tradition, like bonsai?
Growing bulbs hydroponically has been popular for a long time but succulents and cacti hydroculture has only ever been a small subculture.

What is the inspiration behind your designs?
Rather than botany, our designs are based on natural history and specimens. The growth and change in a plant is always something more than we ever could imagine. TERRA products are about showing the contrast of geometric-framed shapes alongside organic plant shapes.

Are there any Japanese arts or techniques that influence your work?
When we combine vessels with plants, it is a similar exploration to bonsai or ikebana, which are inspired by seasons and fables. We use the ideas of *ikeru* (arranging flowers to show the vitality of life) and *mitate* (arranging flowers and plants to convey a fable or landscape). We are also inspired by the Japanese art of *sui seki*, which is about arranging stones to imitate nature and landscapes. By changing the perspective of an object, one has to use their imagination to notice the beauty or strength of nature not previously observed. When we create our pieces, we always have in mind that our main purpose is to create the framework (terrarium/specimen box) for the main characters (plants and stones). Stones

Opposite: 10^{12} TERRA's 'Hanging Argyle' display features English ivy growing in water. English ivy can happily live like this for long periods of time.

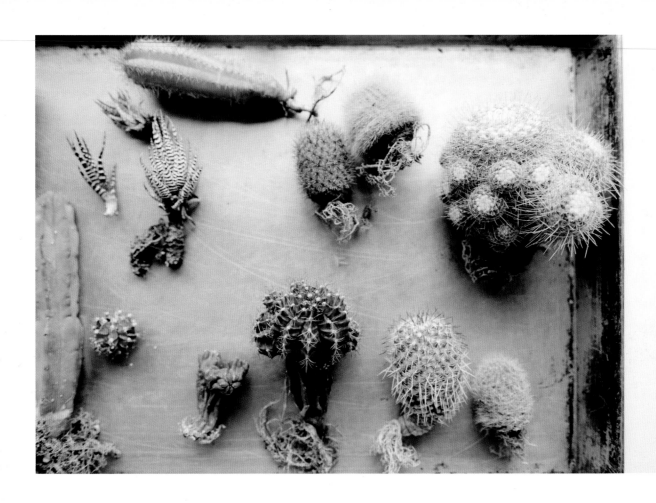

Above: A selection of cacti waiting to be used in 10¹² TERRA pieces.

Opposite: A staghorn fern hangs from the ceiling.

p. 160: The Xerographica airplant hanging from the ceiling needs a good dunk in water on a regular basis and to dry out in between. The Council tree in the pot is a species that is common in Japan although less well-known in other countries as a houseplant.

p. 161, clockwise from top left: Daisuke and Kenichi in Daisuke's apartment which also acts as 10¹² TERRA's studio; 10¹² TERRA's specimen cases on display, along with a Pachypodium species planted in a wooden planter; Daisuke at work in the studio.

on the side of the road or dried flowers express time, history, love and melancholy. Changing our point of view by decorating with these objects gives our small boxes infinite possibilities.

Do you both have many houseplants in your homes?
We both live in apartments and don't have a garden or outdoor space, so all our plants are indoor plants. We both have plants that we like as well as some plants that we are experimenting with for future TERRA products.

What can one enjoy most about growing plants with hydroculture?
We believe that observing a plant daily is important. Then you will notice what the plant needs and start to understand its character. This is what is most enjoyable about hydroculture.

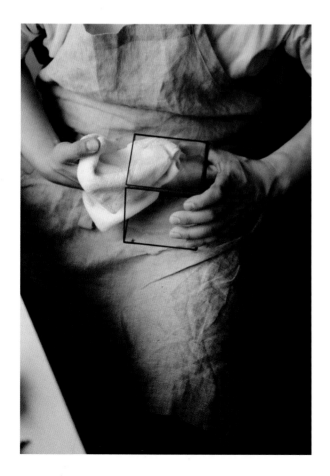

The garden within – Japanese *tsubo niwa*

Marc Peter Keane

Marc Peter Keane is an American landscape architect, artist and writer who lived in Kyoto for 18 years. During this time, he was a research fellow at Kyoto University and later worked as a landscape architect and writer. He is the author of multiple books on Japanese gardens. Here he explores the deeper meaning of a quintessentially Japanese garden — the tsubo niwa.

Tsubo niwa means enclosed garden, or courtyard garden in Japanese. The tsubo niwa can be found in old Japanese shops, in temple buildings, or rambling old houses. It is traditionally contained inside a building, like a jewel in a box and is formed in the tiny 'leftover' space surrounded by adjacent rooms. Tending to a tsubo niwa is a calming and enlivening experience; and the therapeutic nature of this daily ritual illuminates the spiritual benefits of living with an indoor garden.

'Niwa' simply means garden. However 'tsubo' has multiple meanings, depending on how it is written in Japanese. One meaning of 'tsubo' is an area equal to two tatami mats or about 3.3 square metres. Most tsubo niwa are small, some only a few square metres, so this definition implies that the garden is very, very small.

Another way of writing 'tsubo' has a spiritual connotation. To my knowledge, this way of writing 'tsubo' is not used in connection with gardens although it seems the most fitting. There is a belief, in most countries influenced by Chinese culture, in *ki* or 'life energy', which is the force that flows through all things. The concept of *ki* involves pressure points that can be manipulated to invigorate the flow of life energy – such as the needles of acupuncture or the finger pressure of shiatsu. In Japanese, these pressure points are called 'tsubo'. Within a building, the tsubo niwa acts as a point of refreshment to those who live or work in the building. Passing by the garden or sitting by it during a quiet moment in the day, one feels invigorated. In this way it is like the *ki* 'tsubo' of the body. A building is much like the body; life flows through it over time so in its own quiet way, the tsubo niwa can also have a powerful effect on the people who live with it. It is a wellspring of quiet harmony.

Tsubo niwa are not places 'out there' that one goes to stroll in – they are integrally connected with the architecture and life going on inside. They are a tiny point of calm and beauty that become a part of one's daily life; and like most things in life, one must avoid overdoing these gardens. The tsubo niwa is a lesson in reserve and its daily care is made easy by three basic elements of design: simplicity, smallness and proximity. Tsubo niwa are essentially abstracted fragments of nature and their calming effect is made all the more powerful by simple arrangement. Size is also a careful consideration and the tiny size of the tsubo niwa makes it accessible and manageable. Lastly, the arrangement of the tsubo niwa, entirely enclosed by rooms or garden walls, lends a sense of immediacy.

In one example of tsubo niwa I have seen, four or five stems of bamboo rose almost vertically with tufts of leaves clustered at the top. A large stone lantern basked in the light that poured in from above, while at its foot a cherub-faced carving smiled wisely. It was a very simple arrangement and immaculately kept with the gravel on the ground spotless and the wooden floors facing the garden showing a soft sheen from years of daily washing. The whole depicted a sense of loving care.

Most tsubo niwa take less than 15 minutes a day to sweep and water, but in that short time you become connected to the garden. Through this ritual cleaning, the calm of the garden becomes the calm of your heart, and the calm of your heart shows in the garden. To have your own tsubo niwa, whatever form it may take, and leave the work to someone else would be to rob yourself of the best part.

Opposite: Yoshida family residence *tsubo niwa*.
Photo by Marc Peter Keane.

Japanese space. For example, if you re-plant the cactus into a different vessel they can be easily adapted to a space. Certain Japanese types of clay breathe well and I think these pots help cacti and succulents (plants that are not traditionally Japanese) adapt into a traditional Japanese space. Not only with the cactus but with all plants, it is important to always show the best aspect of that plant. If plants are placed one centimetre differently, the whole appearance is different. I display these plants thinking of the whole space.

Do you have plants in your own living space?
Although this is my work, I do not have many plants at home. Only a few in the *tokonoma*.

[This is a traditional architectural feature in a Japanese house and is a recess or alcove, typically a few inches above floor level, for displaying flowers, pictures and ornaments.]

How important are the courtyards at either end of the shop for the interior experience?
The most important thing about a garden is that you can experience all the seasons. I am grateful that in Japan there are four seasons (*shiki*). The fresh green spring, the deeper greens of summer, the red leaves of autumn, the falling leaves of winter. Depending on the season, I hope our customers inside can feel the sun, temperature, wind and the smell of the soil from our garden.

The taste for indoor plants

Julian Patterson

Julian Patterson is one half of Mr Kitly and an architect with a background of research related to aesthetics in architecture. Here Julian draws on a historical perspective to investigate what it means to take aesthetic pleasure in indoor plants.

In May 1952, *The Architectural Review*, an architectural journal of global influence, published a special issue dedicated to indoor plants. The issue included a historical overview of the 'taste for indoor plants', information on species and cultivation, and discussion of their 'uses' addressed principally to designers and architects. The issue reveals the popularity of indoor plants in the post-war period and the extent to which they were considered in the work of design professionals at the time. It is also interesting for the broader historical link it draws between the taste for indoor plants and ideas about aesthetics originating in the 18th century; ideas which offer perspective on our own enthusiasm for plants in interiors today.

In his contribution to the issue, landscape architect and historian H. F. Clarke traces a lineage of English books on indoor plants as far back as the early 17th century. Clarke links this early enthusiasm to new literary and aesthetic fashions, and a taste for the sublime and the picturesque over classical beauty. The pursuit of plant collecting, initially a hobby for the wealthy who could afford it, became a mark of taste embraced by the middle classes. It followed that horticultural books published during those periods provided both practical instruction on cultivation and instruction on taste.

This special issue of *The Architectural Review* follows the same pattern of instruction, both practical and aesthetic. In addition to horticultural guidance, indoor plant selection and arrangement are discussed in terms of decoration and as part of the skillset of designers and architects. Skill in arranging plants, it was argued, was not a matter of rules, but of feelings aroused, in part, by the visual qualities of the plant: 'qualities nearly as impelling as anything devised by a sculptor or a painter'. It is even suggested that the geometric qualities of certain species might have affinities with specific periods or movements in design. For example, it is argued that the geometrical precision of the Rubber plant endeared it to Bauhaus architects in the early 20th century.

For 18th century picturesque theorists, the important thing was to recognise 'painterly' qualities in an object or scene, rather than meaning, or interest in the object itself. Even the most prosaic and distasteful objects might be considered aesthetically pleasing to the disinterested observer with a painterly eye. This kind of observation was meant as a kind of training in aesthetic acuity which could be applied to high art. In its special issue on indoor plants, *The Architectural Review* seems to suggest this same acuity be directed to interior design. Continuity with tradition is emphasised and the reader is assured that the modern interior need not preclude the use of indoor plants as decorative, visual elements in an artful composition.

Picturesque theory was also significant for the idea that there could be a variety of ways of seeing things. Even the mess of ordinary everyday life might be looked at in a different way and brought into the realm of high art conceptually. This thinking influenced surrealism in the 20th century and has had lasting impact seen in an enthusiasm for the found object, permitting the value-free juxtaposition of high art and the everyday as objects of aesthetic appreciation.

This understanding of the picturesque has a different nuance and reflects a different attitude to plants in interiors. Part of the appeal of indoor plants stems from a sense of freedom from value and meaning. Plants offer natural form, un-designed and uncomplicated by questions of style, and there is appeal in the unplanned, when plants take over, or surprise us in unexpected ways.

The Architectural Review states that 'any green living plant is pleasant to look at'. But are there broader implications? Indoor plants might be artfully employed to add colour and form to decor, however sometimes this kind of picturesque scenography can be hollow and, well, just a bit too

nice. There can be a sense of ambivalence when indoor plants are used to project a kind of lifestyle image or symbol of taste, for example in advertising. Equally, the surreal is prone to 'over-ripening' into kitsch once we acclimatise to it and the curiously banal becomes insipid.

Architectural historian and cartoonist, Osbert Lancaster captures these conflicted feelings in his tongue-in-cheek, yet affectionate caricature of the post-war fashion for indoor plants published in the 1953 edition of his book, *Home Sweet Homes*, in which other ubiquitous objects of taste and style – Paul Klee water-colours, Henry Moore drawings and objets trouvés – are dimly discernible through the tangled undergrowth of an indoor jungle. Likewise, British songwriting duo, Flanders and Swann, saw the absurd side of the contemporary taste for indoor plants in their 1957 song, 'Design for Living', when they sang: 'the garden's full of furniture … and the house is full of plants!'

Underlying these apparent jibes, however, is a sensitivity to context, history and traditions, which informs picturesque sensibility. This aesthetic, at once both critical and affectionate, ensures that indoor plants continue to play a part, in ever-changing ways, in everybody's own personal artwork – their home.

Love and
loss and vines

Location
Aspendale, Melbourne, Australia
Residents
Irene Selzer, Peter Selzer,
and their young children
Rueben and Gene
Occupations
Designers, makers, artists,
part-time wine merchant
Place
Home and studio
Plant density
High
Light level
Indirect bright
Plant list
Heartleaf philodendron
Devil's ivy
English ivy
Airplant
Chain of hearts
Aloe vera
Spider plant
Orchid

Irene and Peter Selzer live with their children Rueben and Gene in an art deco period home in a seaside suburb 28 kilometres from Melbourne. They started their design business Iggy and Lou Lou in 2003, making jewellery and homewares. Irene has a Masters of Ceramics and makes the Iggy and Lou Lou pieces in their home studio. Their porcelain skulls are emblematic of their work and are classic art world symbols of love and loss. Iggy and Lou Lou's singular aesthetic and their exploration of themes such as love and loss and life and death have an interesting correlation to the cycles of growth, decay and regeneration in plant life.

What is your philosophy of making?
Our philosophy is make what you love and hopefully it sells so you can keep going! We enjoy making things and getting our hands dirty. People have commented that they wear our jewellery like talismans or amulets. Different plants and flowers consistently feature in each collection. Vases and pots feature predominantly in our home ware collections as we like bringing more of the outside inside.

Your vines are amazing. How did the vines begin, and why vines?
Vines began once we renovated our bathroom. We were going to use wallpaper but weren't confident about the choice of pattern so we started growing a vine-like wallpaper. We have always liked vines – they seem more mysterious to us than other houseplants. You don't know where they are going to go – they surprise you. They're a bit like music, artwork or ideas. They grow and move in different ways. They can surround you and feel magical and they're a bit anthropomorphic in the way they intertwine and join up.

How have they developed and have they needed any special care to get to where they are?
The Heartleaf philodendron puts out feet and almost glues itself to the wall. First it started heading straight up but we wanted it to fill the wall before it hit the ceiling so we threaded the heads back through its stems to make it zig-zag. We also used some small lock hooks to help the variegated leaf vine (Devil's ivy) attach to the wall, as it hasn't put its feet out.

What is your approach to houseplant care?
Look around. If plants look happy don't water them. If they don't look happy, water them. We also give them nutrients twice a year.

Is there any plant that has taken you by surprise in any way?
I have been surprised that outside orchid cuttings can happily live inside for years in vases of water.

Is there a houseplant you have struggled with?
I struggled with the Heartleaf philodendron in the bathroom at the start as I was over-watering. The leaves were all curling and browning. The 'man from the market' said I was drowning it so I started giving it only a cup of water when it was all dry.

Do you have any favourite vessels to house your plant life?
I seem to always be making something on the side to accommodate a new-found plant or cutting. I have also done some great swaps with incredible ceramic and glass artists and had quite a bit of luck picking up great finds at op shops and markets.

Opposite: Irene's studio features a lovingly trained Devil's ivy creeping across the ceiling. This plant was propagated from cuttings taken from the mother plant in the bathroom.

Opposite, left: The detailed world of Iggy and Lou Lou on show. English ivy cutting is planted on top right.

p. 174, left: Heartleaf philodendron making its way across the bathroom wall. It's six years old and started from a small plant.

p. 175, right: Spider plant set off to perfection on a metal pedestal.

Where or how have you learnt most things you know about houseplants?
Talking to plant growers at markets and through books I've collected from top shops, mainly those published in the 1970s and 80s.

Do you have a favourite plant here or one that is extra special to you and why?
I can't pick just one because all of our plants remind me of different things. I especially like swapping cuttings with friends and family because they come with extra personality.

Are plants still beautiful to you when they die?
It's the evolving I love, the connection to the universe over the passage of time. There is never an end with death. There's a real beauty in that. That's why I like looking at plants and things that grow. Plant energy is like people

energy– it's ongoing. Bits that have ended still help new bits to grow. In a similar way there's never really an end to the creative process. It's a living thing and a bit like the way plants evolve. I'm not completely sure where my paintings and sculptures are going to go or where they will stop and I like that.

Your work sometimes references the idea of love and loss. Could you elaborate on the connections between love, loss and plants?
Life and death are opposites of the same coin. You can't have one without the other. There is beauty and sadness in everything. To me it's a balance of love and loss. Within love and loss the love is what is paramount. Love is a big deal to me. The French phrase (*la petite mort*) refers to an aspect of love as a small death. It relates to otherworldly states of being, but

paradoxically it's also about feeling grounded and connected to the universe. Kind of when the world seems massive and small at the same time. Plants have that thing – a connection to the universe, which also reminds you to celebrate the passage of time and just be. They remind you to enjoy each stage and season. Love, plants and art magnify the consciousness of just being. There's so much beauty, magic and mystery in that, which is what I like to explore in my work.

What would be your ultimate artwork involving houseplants?
One of our Heartleaf philodendron vines has put its feet on our painting and is starting to embed itself into the canvas. I'd like to do a series of paintings (and possibly ceramics) with plants embedding themselves like this.

Plant
portraits

Fruit salad plant

Species name
Monstera deliciosa
Family name
Araceae
Light
Prefers indirect bright light,
but tolerates darker positions

The majestic and robust *Monstera deliciosa* is the first houseplant I became really attached to. Although first given its Latin name in 1849, it reached heights of popularity as a houseplant in the early 20th century. Photographs from that time indicate it was a favourite among artists, with towering Monstera featuring in images of the studios of Matisse, Sonia Delaunay and Picasso. Originating in Central America and the West Indies, it is a jungle giant that retains some of its wild nature when brought inside.

The *Monstera's* aerial roots and magnificent large lobed leaves make it a striking specimen but it can be tolerant of pretty tough conditions, surviving long periods of neglect and poor light. It is slow-growing but vigorous, with aerial roots that attach to its surrounding habitat. It grows vertically, attaching itself to tree trunks in the wild, but indoors requires supporting on moss poles or stakes to keep it upright and prevent stem damage under its own weight. It can grow up to 2 metres indoors with leaves 50 centimetres wide. The aerial roots are a sign of a healthy plant and should not be removed but ideally encouraged by attaching to organic matter such as a moss-covered pole or tree branch, as they carry food and water back to the leaves. Outdoors the *Monstera* will produce an edible *delicosa* seed pop, said to be pineapple flavoured. (The rest of the plant should not be eaten and in fact, like many houseplants, can be quite toxic if ingested by pets).

Training your *Monstera* up a moss-covered stake, and giving it good humidity, enough light and moderate water will result in a magnificent, large-leaved specimen. It is a long-lived plant and will be with you for decades.

Growing conditions

Monsteras prefer indirect bright light. They will tolerate low light positions (250–800 lux) but will not grow as well. Try giving it brief spells in a lighter spot. A jungle plant, the *Monstera* loves humidity and warm temperatures (10 to 25 °C), but will tolerate dryer air. Maintain humidity by mist spraying regularly and/or standing on a tray or plate of damp pebbles.

Support

A sturdy stake covered with sphagnum moss makes an ideal scaffold to support the *Monstera*. Add wire mesh around the stake, then attach the moss by pushing it though the mesh. The plant will need securing to its stake with plant ties as it grows. When repotting, the stake is best inserted first before adding the plant and potting mix. Use a tall stake to allow for future growth. Mist the moss pole regularly to encourage the aerial roots to attach themselves to it. The stems of the plant may also be supported using ties, or strings suspended from the ceiling or adjacent wall.

Water and food

Water freely in summer and during hot weather, but never allow it to become waterlogged. Allow it to dry out between watering, especially in winter. Feed as needed during the growing season in spring and summer, but do not feed in autumn or winter.

General care and maintenance

Use a soft cloth dampened with water to wipe off dust and dirt from leaves regularly and pop it in the shower every now and again. Remove any dead or dying leaves at the leaf joints. If the plant gets too big, you can cut off the top just above a node. It will reshoot horizontally. The cutting can be used to propagate a new plant.

Propagation

Monstera can be propagated in early summer via stem tip cutting. Cuttings will also root readily in water and can then be potted.

Troubleshooting

Black patches on the leaves may indicate conditions are too cold or draughty. Yellowing then browning leaves may mean over-watering. Allow the plant to dry out between watering and water less often. Pale yellow leaves are a sign of chlorosis, usually caused by a lack of nutrients or over-watering. Webs underneath the leaves indicate red spider mite.

Devil's ivy

Species name
Epipremnum aureum
Family name
Araceae
Light
Prefers indirect bright light,
but tolerates darker positions

The *Epipremnum aureum*, or Devil's ivy, is a one of the most commonly kept houseplants in the world. With a relatively recent (1964) accepted Latin name, a rise to heady heights of popularity in office decor of the 1980s, and no consensus on where it actually originated until 2004 (an island in French Polynesia called Moorea), Devil's ivy is a very modern houseplant. It is so common as to border on ubiquitous and can be seen tumbling over the edge of filing cabinets and traipsing along windowsills worldwide.

Originating in tropical Asia, the *Epipremnum aureum* is a fast-growing, epiphytic climber with self-clinging stems. In a hot and humid jungle it can grow up to 15 metres and produce huge leaves. Indoors, in a dryer and cooler environment, it will curb its enthusiasm a little and rarely exceed 2 metres. It has both terrestrial and aerial roots. Aerial roots cling to trees providing both support and additional nourishment. In pots it requires support to stay upright. It is happiest attached to moss poles or other organic matter, without which growth can slow and the aerial roots shrivel as the plant depends on terrestrial roots alone for nutrients. Devil's ivy belongs to same family of hardy indoor plants as Monstera, Philodendron and Syngonium, and is also often referred to as Golden pothos or by its superseded botanical name *Scindapsus aureus*. Its variegated alternate leaves are marbled green and lemony yellow, differentiating it from the Philodendron heart-leaf climber of the same family.

It's a perfect for houseplant beginners as it can cope with some neglect and wide-ranging conditions. Trail it over a mantelpiece, pin it across walls, train it up a screen or hang it up high – Devil's ivy gives endless options. It's also a top-rated air purifier, absorbing an array of indoor airborne pollutants. A modern classic.

Growing conditions
Devil's ivy will survive a wide range of environmental conditions, but grows best at 10 to 25 °C. It likes high humidity so mist spray regularly in summer. It will tolerate low light (250–800 lux) but prefers indirect bright light (800–1600 lux).

Water and food
In summer keep plants moist but not waterlogged, and in winter allow to dry out more. Be careful of over-watering and use tepid water. Feed with soluble indoor plant food a few times throughout spring and summer. If the aerial roots can be attached to moss poles or other organic support it will grow more quickly.

General care and maintenance
Clean the leaves with a damp sponge regularly, Misting also helps to clean the leaves. Remove any yellowing or decaying leaves. Repot in spring or summer into good draining soil that retains moisture. Prune at any time just above a leaf node if the plant is getting too rampant.

Propagation
Devil's ivy can be propagated via stem cuttings in spring and summer. Snip 15 centimetres off the tips of any overly eager trailing stems and use these cuttings to propagate. Cut with a sharp knife just above a leaf node, then cut again just below the next node and plant in propagation mix. Cuttings will also grow roots in water and can then be potted on into soil.

Troubleshooting
Devil's ivy is a good pest-resistant plant. Brown spots on leaves indicate it is being kept too cold and over-watered. Vines with very long gaps between leaves usually lack adequate light, so move to a brighter position.

Planter note: Basketball hanger
by Sarah Parkes (Smalltown).

Boston fern

Species name
Nephrolepis exaltata
Family name
Nephrolepidaceae
Light
Prefers indirect bright light,
but tolerates darker positions

Nephrolepis exaltata has been a popular houseplant in England for centuries, largely because it could tolerate cold, poorly lit interiors and the fumes of early Victorian heating systems. Interest in ferns as houseplants in Britain began in earnest in the late 1830s when increasing numbers of amateur botanists began to roam the British countryside in search of new fern species. By 1855, natural history enthusiast and friend of Charles Darwin, Charles Kingsley, had coined the term 'pteridomania', meaning fern madness. He noted to parents of the time, 'Your daughters, perhaps, have been seized with the prevailing 'pteridomania', and are collecting and buying ferns, with Ward's cases wherein to keep them (for which you have to pay)' (Boyd, 1992).

Nephrolepis exaltata originates in the tropics and sub-tropics, extending to temperate Japan and New Zealand, and was first named in 1838. The genus of around forty different species of ferns has become universally known as the Boston fern because of the enormous popularity of *Nephrolepis exaltata bostoniensis*. This was a 19th-century cultivar discovered in Boston, Massachusetts, which became particularly popular for its characteristic arching fronds. The Boston fern is also known under the other common names of Sword fern or Fishbone fern. It's classified as a weed in many countries due to its ability to spread and naturalise via runners. New growth appears from the centre of the plant, which can double in size in a year given ideal growing conditions, reaching huge proportions with fronds up to 1.5 metres long. Given enough moisture and humidity, it is a very easy houseplant to care for and will cope with some low light.

Placed on a pedestal or hanging from above, the Boston fern's luminously green, softly drooping fronds have a soft grace and charm that belies the plant's toughness. This Victorian-era parlour favourite brings a nostalgic atmosphere and timeless elegance to any room.

Growing conditions

Boston ferns prefer indirect bright light (800–1600 lux) and should always be protected from any direct sun. They will endure darker positions but will not thrive. They like high humidity (assisted by a daily mist spray) and love the bathroom as long as temperatures stay between 11 and 24 °C. They will suffer in dry conditions and do not like draughts or blasts of heat.

Water and food

Boston ferns need to be kept moist, so check the soil moisture regularly. Make sure the plant has good drainage to prevent waterlogging. In winter or cool temperatures allow to dry out a little more between waterings. They prefer rainwater. Feed every two to four weeks with a soluble foliar spray or liquid fertiliser during the growth season in spring and summer. Boston ferns prefer fertiliser suitable for acid-loving plants.

General care and maintenance

Mist spraying helps keeps the foliage clean and popping it outside in the rain or under a cold/tepid shower will help refresh the plant. Prune off any dead fronds. Particularly long fronds can be pruned back as necessary. Boston ferns can get quite big and if you want them to keep growing bigger they will need potting on every one to two years in spring. Use potting mix suitable for acid-loving plants.

Propagation

Boston ferns can be propagated by detaching plantlets that grow on the end of little runners near the base of the plant. They can also be propagated by division.

Troubleshooting

Poor coloration of fronds and no new growth usually means the plant needs feeding or repotting. Yellowing of fronds (chlorosis) may mean too much bright light, or under- or over-watering, Remove from any direct sun and check the watering regime and drainage. Drooping and brittle leaves may mean that the atmosphere or soil is too dry.

Planter note: Mr Kitly curved ceiling hanger.

Ficus alii

Species name
Ficus maclellandii King
Family name
Moraceae
Light
Prefers indirect bright light,
but tolerates darker positions

Ficus maclellandii King is a slender-leaved, tree-like plant originating in India. This attractive yet relatively underused houseplant is a great example of the, at times, tortuous and circulatory world of botanical nomenclature. From what I can establish, the original species, *Ficus maclellandii* King, is named after a British botanist George King, who worked in the Royal Botanical Garden in Calcutta in British India from 1871 until his death in 1909. This is an accepted name according to most reputable botanical resources such as *The Plant List*.

The common name most often applied to this plant, Ficus alii, makes multiple appearances (hence the common name!) and is certainly in regular use at the expense of an accepted Latin name at plant nurseries in Australia. This common name override may indicate that this particular plant is a new cultivar of the original *Ficus maclellandii* King. New houseplants cultivar names have always been hard to keep track of and often the marketing imperative to legitimise a name of a new cultivar leaps ahead of the more cautious and thorough botanical name checks. Perhaps with the rise of online information and sales of houseplants, the eternal problem of botanical mis-naming is gradually being compounded. There a few unsubstantiated online accounts that the 'alii' appellation comes from the Hawaiian term 'Ali 'I' which translates as 'chief' or 'king'. These accounts link the plant to recent commercial production in Hawaii. But that strikes me as a possible conflation with the accepted species name (given in 1887) of *Ficus maclellandii* King.

The Ficus alii naturally grows as multiple slender branches, but can be pruned into a ball on top. Outside in the ground it can grow to 3 metres tall, while potted it will reach around 2 metres. The slender, olive-coloured leaves can grow to 20 centimetres long. Other Ficus varieties have led the charge in terms of popular houseplants, the *Ficus benjamina* (Weeping fig) and the *Ficus elastica* (Rubber plant) to name but two. The recent increasing popularity of the Ficus alii may be in part due to its tolerance of varied conditions and as an added bonus it doesn't drop it leaves as readily as the fussier *Ficus benjamina*. The plant's slender drooping foliage lends it a whimsical, sighing air. This mercurial quality is perhaps reflected in the search for its right name.

Growing conditions
The Ficus alii is best located in indirect bright light (800–1600 lux), but will tolerate lower light (250–800 lux). It prefers temperatures between 10 and 24 °C, but will tolerate down to 7 °C for short periods of time. It likes an occasional mist spray to increase humidity.

Water and food
Keep plants moist in hot weather but otherwise keep on the drier side and allow the top half of the pot to dry out inbetween, especially in winter or cold weather. Water well and less often is key here. Tepid water is better than the shock of ice-cold water. Feed monthly while growing during spring and summer.

General care and maintenance
Misting helps to keep plants clean. A shower outdoors will do the same. Wipe the leaves clean with a damp cloth as necessary. You can give it a trim with pruning shears any time to control the size of the plant. Cut the stems just above a leaf or stem. Remove any dead branches or weak growth. The roots are slow growing, filling the pot around every two years. Pot on in spring.

Propagation
Propagate by taking stem cuttings in summer. It can be difficult, as the cuttings need to be kept warm to establish. Be sure to keep in a sunny warm spot indoors. A propagation heat mat is recommended.

Troubleshooting
Ficus alii is a fairly pest-resistant and trouble-free plant all round, but can be susceptible to scale. Leaf drop may occur if it is located in draughts or near heating or cooling vents, or if the plant is over-watered.

Planter note: Sharon Alpren bronze ceramic planter from Mr Kitly.

Kentia palm

Species name
Howea forsteriana
Family name
Arecaceae
Light
Prefers indirect bright light,
but tolerates darker positions

The Kentia palm is from Lord Howe Island, a small island that is part of Australia and situated in the Tasman Sea. Palms were a fashionable addition to the conservatories of the well-to-do in Britain, Europe and the US. The use of palms as decorative motifs in interiors peaked worldwide with the emergence of the glass atrium palm courts of prestigious hotels in the 19th century. Lord Howe Island was settled in 1834 and by the 1870s the islanders turned to the collection and export of Kentia palm seeds to the booming European indoor plant market to support the local economy. The popularity of the Kentia as houseplants grew, as a result of their graceful shape and ability to tolerate the low light and dry conditions of indoors. They are one of the most successful and popular houseplants in the world.

Nowadays the trade in Kentia palm seeds is well-regulated and remains an important source of revenue for the tiny World Heritage-listed island. For the first 100 years of the plant's commercial development, it was only sold as seed. Since the 1980s the islanders have been growing tree seedlings for export. The seeds are gathered from the island's natural forests and profit from sales of the plants worldwide is returned to the island to assist in managing its natural ecosystems. Thus the Kentia is a good choice for Australian houseplant enthusiasts with a sustainable frame of mind. It's a native plant that makes a perfect houseplant, as opposed to the many introduced species that, while very popular when contained as cultivated houseplants, have become problematic weeds in the wild in their adopted countries.

The Kentia has erect stems and arching fronds, and is a slow-growing palm that will eventually grow to 3 metres in pots, or as high as 20 metres in the wild. It's a tough houseplant that belies its sense of glamour. Coping well with low light, they epitomise the classy toughness of all palms. In 1952, *The Architectural Review* said they 'thrive on the tea dregs and the unequivocal airs of hotel lounges and ballrooms'.

The Kentia palm is the go-to option for adding a certain lush formality to interiors. A symbol of bygone opulence, it has made its tiny island home famous. It's perhaps a little jaded but ready for a comeback.

Growing conditions
Kentia palms can tolerate darker positions (250–800 lux) but prefer indirect bright light (800–1600 lux). They are comfortable at temperatures between 10 and 24 °C. Kentias enjoy a shower in the rain and regular mist sprays. They are intolerant of draughts.

Water and food
In summer and hot weather keep regularly moist, watering at least a couple of times a week. Liquid fertilise every couple of weeks during the summer for optimum growth. Feeding is not required during winter.

General care and maintenance
A mist spray helps to keep the palms clean. Wipe all over, including stems, with a clean damp sponge. Repot in spring once a year if necessary. Deep pots are best. Remove any dead or dying leaves with a sharp cut at their base. You can also trim off any browning tips. Cut on an angle to give a more 'natural' appearance.

Troubleshooting
Browning leaf tips usually indicate the room is too dry so increase the humidity. If the entire leaf browns it may mean that the plant has dried out too much. No new growth indicates it needs feeding and a repot. The palms are susceptible to scale and red spider mite. Over-watering (usually in winter) will result in the plant rotting and blackening at the base.

Heartleaf philodendron

Species name
Philodendron hederaceum

Family name
Araceae

Light
Prefers indirect bright light,
but tolerates darker positions

Originally collected and named by Viennese botanist Heinrich Willhelm Schott in the 1830s, the *Philodendron hederaceum* was the centre of a 180-year argument over its correct designation. Over time, botanists realised that the quite varied specimens they were studying belonged to the same species. Its common name derives from the shape of its leaves, known as cordate, meaning 'leaf that is shaped like a heart'. Originating in the Solomon Islands, it naturally grows very high in trees and trails towards the jungle floor as a hanging vine. It belongs to a very large genus with all Philodendron being some of the easiest plants to keep as houseplants. They are an exceedingly versatile and tolerant bunch, and given half a chance they will all climb. These plants are literally tree hugging as the name Philodendron derives from the Greek 'philo' (love) and 'dendron' (tree).

The Heartleaf philodendron is a vigorous, epiphytic, fast-growing climber with vining stems and heart-shaped leaves. Leaves can reach 40 centimetres long in the wild, but will remain much smaller indoors at around 10 centimetres. The vining stems can grow up to 1 metre in a year. It has both terrestrial and aerial roots. In the wild its aerial roots cling to trees or organic matter, providing both support and additional nourishment. In pots they require support to stay upright and, like Devil's ivy, are happiest attached to moss-covered poles or other organic matter such as a tree branch. Otherwise growth can slow and the aerial roots shrivel as the plant depends on terrestrial roots alone.

The Heartleaf philodendron is one of my all-time favourite houseplants. It can be trained up canes, draped from hanging baskets, and pinned across walls and around windows. It is one of the very hardiest and easiest climbing plants to grow indoors. A keeper.

Growing conditions

Heartleaf philodendrons will endure low light (250–800 lux) but prefer indirect bright light (800–1600 lux). They prefer a temperature range of 14 to 24 °C and appreciate a regular mist spray.

Water and food

Keep plants moist in summer, but not waterlogged. Allow to dry out more between waters in winter. Feed regularly during the growing season in spring and summer.

General care and maintenance

Heartleaf philodendrons enjoy a regular shower. Clean the leaves regularly with a damp soft cloth and remove dead leaves at the stem. They can be repotted every year in early summer. Top dress large plants that are too unwieldy to repot with new potting mix or compost. They can be pruned as desired by snipping off 15 centimetres from the tips of trailing stems.

Propagation

Heartleaf philodendrons can be propagated by cutting a leaf tip or stem section in summer. Use a stem tip cutting with a healthy growing tip and at least two healthy leaves, or a stem section with at least two nodes. The plant can also be propagated in water to grow roots then potted on into soil.

Troubleshooting

Drooping leaves means the plant is too dry, so give a good soak. Poor leaf colour and no new growth at all may mean it needs to be in a warmer spot, have fresh potting mix or more regular feeding. Yellowing leaves are often the symptom of over-watering, particularly in winter. Allow plants to dry out and water less often. Brown edges may be a sign of scorch. Chlorosis is somewhat common. Usually an increase in iron or magnesium will help.

Planter note: Mr Kitly steel plant stand with Tara Shackell plant stand bowl

Pony tail palm

Species name
Beaucarnea guatemalensis Rose
Family name
Asparagaceae
Light
Bright light to indirect bright light

The Pony tail palm is not actually a palm, but a small tropical tree originally from Central and South America. The Asparagaceae family it belongs to includes other popular houseplants such as Mother-in-law's tongue, the *Yucca* and *Aspidistra*, all equally tough and forgiving plants. The *Beaucarnea guatemalensis* Rose is a rarer species than the more commonly kept houseplant *Beaucarnea recurvate*. It's native to Guatemala and was given its Latin name by American botanist Joseph Nelson Rose in 1906. Pony tail palms have been something of a sleeper in terms of houseplant popularity, especially when compared to the evergreen popularity of their lush tropical foliage competitors or the multifarious cactus forms that provoke a tendency to collect. But they are here for the long haul and their easy care is reward for the houseplant fan who bucks the trends.

The Pony tail palm is one of the toughest indoor plants you can choose, able to tolerate periods of neglect by storing water in the bottle-like swollen base of its trunk. It's a type of caudiciform, which is a term that describes plants with a fat or swollen trunk. (Caudiciforms need not be botanically related. There are caudiciform cacti, trees and vines, all species from many different genera.) In its natural habitat the swollen base of the *Beaucarnea guatemalensis* can reach up to 1.5 metres wide and the tree 9 metres tall, but growth can be controlled in a small pot. It has cascading narrow, strappy and finely serrated leaves up to 2 metres long and 1.5 centimetres wide. New growth has a rose-red blush. Flowers are produced only on older trees and rarely indoors. Slow growing with a small root structure, the Pony tail palm is well-suited to being kept in a small pot for an extended period without needing to pot-on. It is a great option for an easy indoor bonsai and can live for decades.

Something about its long cascading leaves gives this species of Pony tail palm a louche feel that I enjoy. With its striking unusual proportions, I think the *Beaucarnea guatemalensis* deserves to be welcomed more widely into our living spaces.

Growing conditions

Prefers bright (1600 lux and over) to indirect bright light (800–1600 lux). Poor light conditions are tolerated, but may result in weaker, thinner stems. It prefers a warm position and temperatures 10 to 28°C. It can survive lower temperatures, but may lose leaves. It originates from desert areas so can handle dry conditions, but they like a mist spray, and humidity also helps keep pests at bay. Avoid draughts.

Water and food

Water deeply but intermittently. Allow to dry out well between watering just enough to keep the foliage from shrivelling, especially in winter. Water more often in hot dry weather, about once every three weeks, as long as the soil drains well. Over-watering is the number one way to kill this plant. Its swollen trunk stores water, allowing it to survive some periods of neglect, but making it more susceptible to over-watering. Only feed once during the growing season in summer.

General care and maintenance

Any dying lower leaves can be removed. Clean the leaves by wiping with a damp cloth. A mist spray also helps. The plant grows slowly so it can be kept in the same pot for years and growth can be controlled by keeping it in a small pot. If you do repot, use well-draining potting mix such as a good quality cactus mix. Be careful not to damage the base or bury roots too deeply. Roots need to be near the surface when planted. Varied information is available on pruning, but most advise not to do so.

Propagation

Pony tail palms can be propagated from seed if you can source it from specialist seed suppliers or from a dried seed head after flowering. Sow in spring. An easier and faster method is by offsets when they appear at the base of the plant.

Troubleshooting

A good pest resistant plant but keep an eye out for the usual suspects – scale, mealy bug and red spider mite in dry conditions indoors. The plant will rot if over-watered.

Vanda x hybrid orchid

Species name
Vanda

Family name
Orchidaceae

Light
Bright light

Orchids inspire obsession like no other plant. A trail of intense orchid appreciation can be traced from a period of 'Orchidelerium' in Victorian England to recent stories of collecting expeditions driven by love or money. A much longer history of orchid appreciation in Asia is a welcome counterpoint to the generally Euro-centric focus of houseplant history. Orchids have been an important symbol in Chinese culture and art since ancient history. They have been used ornamentally, their fragrance has prompted poems and songs, and the flower symbolises the Confucian qualities of noble integrity. In Japan the native Wind orchid (*Neofinetia falcata*) is posited to be the first orchid to be grown as a houseplant in 17th-century Edo-era Japan. Feudal lords would reportedly seek out the flower in the wild to present to the reigning Shogun and it remains a popular collector's orchid today.

I have developed a particular attachment to keeping the Vanda orchid species indoors since procuring this fine specimen with a mass of meandering tangled aerial roots from a local grower. The Vanda orchid comes from South-East Asia and is a large growing epiphyte with a long aerial roots system and a vine-like growth habit. Vandas can quickly become quite massive in the wild, with root lengths of up to 2 metres. In cultivation they are highly prized for their fragrant flower spikes of intense colour.

Orchids can be enticing plants to have indoors yet are the most difficult, requiring near perfect greenhouse-like conditions. To keep a Vanda orchid (or any orchid for that matter) contentedly green-leafed and with exuberant roots indoors, let alone to get it to flower, requires some special attentions. It needs heat, high humidity, robust airflow, drenching rain and dry spells. I keep my orchid in our rear west-facing sunroom where it gets bright light and warmth, and where we can leave the window open for it to catch the breeze. I water it every other day (less in winter) by giving it a good drench in the shower. I leave it hanging in the shower recess to drip dry before replacing it in its sunroom home to dry out in the breeze. It's demanding, seductive and could potentially become an all-consuming endeavour, but therein lies the charm of the orchid.

Growing conditions
Vanda orchids prefer bright light with some protection from direct sun.

Water and food
Vanda orchids require copious quantities of water in the summer growing season but a drier period to rest in the cooler months. The root colour indicates when watering is required. White means watering required; green means sufficient water has been absorbed. Water by drenching in the shower or outside for around 5 minutes. Do not allow plants to remain wet. They need to dry out in between watering. Vandas are heavy feeders, so follow a regular feeding regime of a soluble fertiliser.

General care and maintenance
Vanda orchids require a temperature of 15 to 32 °C, with an ideal humidity of 80 per cent. Excellent, consistent air movement is key. If you can't keep it somewhere with good air flow, try hanging it outdoors during the day.

Soil and repotting
Grow in very coarse media or entirely bare rooted in plastic pots or suspended open slatted planters. Weave the roots through the slats of the basket and secure the stem with wire. Vandas resent disturbance and if extra support is required put the smaller basket inside a new, bigger basket and let it do its thing.

Troubleshooting
Lack of airflow is the reason for most of the difficulties associated with keeping orchids indoors. As Vandas are grown bare rooted, they are particularly intolerant of fluctuating conditions and can drop lower leaves and have a straggling appearance when unhappy. Yellow or dark spots on leaves are often a sign that you need to up one or all of the essential elements of heat, light, humidity, airflow and water. You may need to move them outdoors in daytime and keep them indoors only at night or in the cold.

Plant care

Perhaps the best piece of general advice for a houseplant enthusiast is to know your plant. In particular know where it comes from and the natural environment in which it thrives. This will always help in determining how best to care for it indoors.

There are some four million different kinds of animals and plants in the world. Four million different solutions to the problems of staying alive.
David Attenborough

Light

All plants need light to thrive. Sunlight is a plant's primary source of energy. Many common houseplants come from jungle and rainforest environments, but even the shady understorey of their native environment can provide a plant with more light than it will ever receive indoors. In nature plant species have adapted in different ways to access enough light for themselves for the process of photosynthesis. For example, the aerial roots and tendrils of the common houseplant genus Philodendron allow it to climb up trees where there is more light.

A good plan when working out what plants will suit your room is to know which way your windows face so you are aware of the light they will receive and can choose plants to suit. Generally any room with a decent-sized and unobstructed north, east or west-facing window, or even better an overhead skylight, should provide enough light for the plants featured in this book to survive. However, it is advisable to be quite aware of the light each will receive for them to be at their best. If plants don't get enough light they won't grow well. But too much direct light on some species and leaves may burn. If all you have available to you is low light consider investigating ways to augment light by using artificial means such as compact fluorescents or LEDs, an area of considerable technological growth in recent times with interesting houseplant installation potential.

Measuring light

A long history of indoor plant lore and terminology comes into play when discussing light conditions for indoor plants. Light intensity has traditionally been defined by houseplant writers in terms of low light, medium/indirect bright light and high/bright light. Light intensity depends on the way the room faces, the size of the window or light source, seasons, weather and any shading. This common parlance tradition can also be enhanced with a bit of physics lite by using the light intensity (or more specifically 'illumination') measurement called lux. Lux is traditionally measured with professional light meters, but recent online app innovations make lux measurement an accessible (if not foolproof) addition to the houseplant enthusiast's toolkit. As a relative measure, natural sunlight outdoors can reach up to around of 32,000–100,000 lux, while indoors can generally range from 20–2000 lux and low light for plants is deemed to be approximately 250–800 lux, with bright light 1600 lux and over. Taking multiple readings over the course of the day (and over the course of the year) will give a more accurate average light reading for your room as light intensity will change depending on weather and seasons and structures/shading.

Light source

High/bright light will be provided by a large unobstructed north- or west-facing window or skylight. Place the plant directly in front of the light source, with periods outdoors where possible for extra light boosts. There should be average lux measurements of 1600 and above. Plants that naturally grow and prefer open sunny spaces such as succulents, Yucca, Crotons, Plumeria, Pony tail palm, Bird of paradise, *Dracaena marginata*, Passionflower and other flowering plants. Also include in this section many of the medium light plants, such as Ficus alii and Rubber plants. They will do better in brighter light provided they get some protection from periods of burning sunlight.

Medium light/indirect bright light will be provided by a north-, east- or west-facing window or skylight. Place plants within a metre or so of the light source, with a sheer curtain or other protection blocking fierce burning sunlight. There should be average lux measurements of 800–1600. A broad range of plants will survive in this light, including most of the popular houseplants such as the Ficus species, including Rubber plants, *Ficus benjamina* and Ficus alii, philodendron species, including Heartleaf philodendron, *Monstera delicosa*, Spider plants, Devil's ivy, English ivy, airplants and other bromeliads, and most palms. Then also include in this category all of the low light plants below. They will generally do better in medium light.

Low light will be provided by a south-facing window, shaded window or placement of plants more than 2 metres from a window. There should be average lux measurements of 250–800 (it is unlikely that any plant will survive below 50 lux). Houseplants that will survive (the notion of survive is key here, no plant will ever really flourish in low light, more accurately they will 'exist') are the Cast-iron plant, Zanzibar gem, Kentia palm, Mother-in-law's tongue, Peace lily, *Dieffenbachia*, *Aglaonema*, Chain of hearts, Corn plant, Lady palm and Devil's ivy.

Keep in mind that light intensity varies with the seasons, so try moving your plants to different positions at different times of the year to suit their preferred light conditions. For example, a Staghorn fern loves direct winter light, but should be protected from direct summer light.

Watering

Many people ask how many times a week to water, but there is no simple answer or a set watering recipe. Watering requirements depend on the plant, and the light, temperature and season. Plants will need more water in hot weather, in a bright window and in summer, and less in cool weather, low light and in winter, when most plants are not growing as fast due to lower light. Most houseplants die from too much watering, they are literally loved to death. It is much more rare for a plant to die from under-watering. Try following these tips to keep your watering regime in check.

Before watering test the potting mix for moisture. Poke a finger in. If it feels dry and crumbly down to a finger's depth you can usually water. If you feel moisture below the surface, give it a little more time to dry out. Another method is to tap the side of the pot or lift it. If it feels heavy it is likely still waterlogged, so let it dry out more before watering again. A dowel or stick poked in and pulled out with soil clinging to it also indicates the plant is still moist down around the root ball and that there's no need to water. Feel is always the best way to get to know and understand your plants. But for technological fun and insight you can also use a moisture meter, available at many hardware stores. New phone apps are also blossoming in this area.

Watering a plant deeply and allowing it to dry out between waters allows the roots to breathe. Water until the water runs from bottom into the drainage tray below. Wait for the plant to soak it back up, but be sure to empty any excess after 10 minutes or so.

Reduce your watering in winter. Plants receive less light during late autumn and winter, and so grow more slowly and require less water. You can usually decrease your watering during this period to just enough to prevent shrivelling.

No one likes wet feet. Choose your potting mix carefully and always use good quality mix that allows for water retention but also for excellent drainage. Drainage can be improved by adding pebbles at the bottom of the pot. If the pot is too big for the plant, the plant's root system might struggle to take up enough of the water and its roots may weaken and rot.

Water quality and temperature is also important. Use room temperature water, and never really cold water to avoid shocking the plants. Try using rainwater, especially for acid-loving plants such as the Boston fern. Chlorine in tap water can build up in the soil of houseplants sometimes to their detriment. Reduce chlorine by leaving tap water to evaporate in an open bucket for a few hours before watering. Another old-fashioned booster technique is to periodically add used tea leaves from your morning brew to the watering can. Tea, especially green tea, has good levels of nitrogen, which is great for plants.

Keep a regular watering schedule and preferably water in the morning to avoid plants sitting in damp conditions overnight when it is colder.

Feeding

Plants in pots will eventually exhaust the nutrients in their potting mix and will need supplementary food. During spring and summer it helps to feed your plant with a dilution of indoor plant suitable fertiliser. Like over-watering, over-feeding can be detrimental, so err on the side of caution. If your plant is already ailing severely, be sure to treat the root cause of the ailment rather than simply fertilise it. Fertiliser is not medicine but meant for strongly growing plants to give them an extra boost. You can feed your plants by diluting the fertiliser in your watering can or via foliar spray with a mister. When repotting or top-dressing your houseplant add in some worm castings or organic compost to give the soil a boost. During the plant's slower growth period in autumn and winter, don't feed it at all.

Temperature

Most common houseplants can cope with an indoor temperature range of 15 to 25 °C. Indoor temperatures consistently below 14 °C may impact the growth or health of the plants and below 10 degrees can often prove fatal. When indoor temperatures rise into the 20s it is best to also increase the level of humidity. As a rule of thumb, comfortably warm temperatures and humid conditions make happy plants.

Indoor plants appreciate constancy in temperature. Keep them away from hot windows in summer and cold windows in winter, and from radiant heaters and blasts of air from heating and cooling vents. More natural, passive and gradual methods of controlling temperature, such as opening and closing windows and using ceiling fans, are preferable to the use of air conditioners, which dry out the air. Avoid sudden extreme temperature changes such as taking plants from outside to inside or vice versa. Use a halfway house such as a shade house or somewhere protected to gradually accustom the plants to the change. Most plants also enjoy a bit of fresh air. Try to position them with access to good ventilation, but avoid draughts. Aim for a buoyant atmosphere, not a cold draughty one.

Humidity

Most of the houseplants in this book come from sub-tropical or tropical climes and so prefer relatively humid conditions. Exceptions are many succulents and cacti and drier desert plants, which do not need such high humidity levels. Humidity is important for plant health and can help to

help keep them cool in hot weather (avoid this for the temperamental Maidenhair fern). Placing your plant on a bed of small pebbles then pouring water in halfway up the depth of the pebbles will also help create a humid microclimate, but never let the water go over the top of the pebbles. Plants hate having their roots sit in water. A shower with tepid water or placing the plant outdoors on a dull day also provides a good humidity burst.

The terrarium was invented to solve this very problem of maintaining adequate humidity and moisture. Bell jar covers, home-made clear glass or plastic plant covers, or purpose-built terrariums are a great way to house small plants with high humidity needs.

noticeable as salt crusts on top of the potting mix or around the edge of the pot, or visible at drainage holes. Do this by pouring tepid water through the potting mix until it drains out freely from the bottom. Repeat a couple of times.

Potting and repotting

You 'pot on' when the plant outgrows its pot, and you 'repot' when you want to do a complete refresh of the plant's soil. Always buy good quality potting mix. It is possible to add a little extra drainage to your mix with sand, or moisture retention using sphagnum moss, depending on the plant. Specialist mixes or common indoor plants are available. Hanging plants, for example, would appreciate water retentive

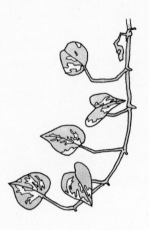

Leaf nodes

Sweet potato growing in water

Repotting

decrease the incidence of mealy bug and other common indoor pests. In general, a good humidity level for plants is 70 to 90 per cent, which is often hard to achieve indoors where relative humidity is more often between 20 and 60 per cent. Heating and cooling systems and air conditioning tend to dry the air too much for most houseplants' pleasure.

How to increase humidity

You can look into buying a humidifier for a technological solution. There are also many basic ways you can increase humidity. A group of plants indoors will actually create their own little microclimate and slightly increase humidity, helping each other out. A mist spray every other day can help keep up humidity for plants that enjoy it and

Cleaning and refreshing

Plants work hard to keep our indoor air clean and pure, so we should return the favour by making sure their leaves are free from dust to enable them to breath easily. Cleaning leaves also helps prevent pests. Clean large leaves using a soft damp cloth and tepid water. Giving plants a good all-over shower at least once a month is good for your plants' general health and wellbeing since it mimics the natural rainfall they would receive outside. Do it up to once a week if you are keen, either in your shower recess or by taking them outside on a warm but overcast day and giving them a good sprinkle with the hose or a wash in the rain. At the same time, it is good to flush out any salts that may have built up in the potting mix from fertilisers,

mix as they dry out quickly. All plants need excellent drainage. You can usually pot-on once a year in spring or summer when the plant is actively growing. Ideally repot into a pot with about 2 to 3 centimetres extra space all around the original in order to keep the root system strong and not have a disproportionate pot and plant scenario. Make sure the potting mix is moist before you begin repotting. You only really need to pot-on once the plant shows signs of becoming pot bound, with roots creeping through the base of the pot. Some plants, such as hoya, Spider plant, and Rubber plant don't mind staying in the same pot and don't need regular potting on. The growth of others can be controlled by being judicious in how often they are potted-on. The Boston fern or the *Monstera delicosa* can become giant if you pot-on every year, but with less regular upgrades their growth can be controlled.

Potting-on

Prepare the new pot with a layer of drainage such as pebbles if you have them then some potting mix (all plants will enjoy the extra drainage help), but if not just put some potting mix in the bottom. Moisten the plant's soil, put your hand over the top of the plant, with your fingers around the stem, invert the pot and gently ease the plant out. (You may need to tap the pot's side to help ease it out.) Shake off a bit of the old potting mix, being careful not to damage the new roots, place the plant in the centre of the new pot and add new potting mix to fill the pot, making sure all roots are covered. Press down firmly.

Repotting

Repotting

Repotting is more for older established pot plants that need freshening up with new potting mix, but don't need to get any bigger. Remove the plant from its original pot. Shake or fork off the soil around the roots and trim back the root ball by about a quarter using a trowel or handfork, or even scissors or a knife for tougher roots. (Don't worry, this will not harm the plant and fresh new roots will grow after repotting.) Replace the plant in its original pot or a new one of same size, along with fresh potting mix all around and under it. If your plant is too big, ungainly or difficult to manoeuvre, you can 'top dress' every spring or summer rather than completely repot. Remove the top inch or so of potting mix and replace with fresh, good quality mix, including some compost if you have it.

Pinching and pruning

Sometimes a houseplant might need to be trimmed back under control. The Devil's ivy for example might happily continue to grow until it fills the room. Prune most plants in spring and summer. For soft stem-climbing plants such as Devil's ivy and Heartleaf philodendron, cut just above a leaf or growth node (where leaves and roots grow from the stem) with pruners or sharp scissors. For large hard-stem plants such as *Dracaena* or *Monstera*, use good quality strong bypass secateurs or a pruning saw and cut the stem just above a leaf node. New shoots will grow from just below the cut. Pinching off the tip of a growing shoot with thumb and forefingers will help get a bushier plant going. This is good for plants such as the Heartleaf philodendron and Devil's ivy.

Plantlets

Propagation

Propagating your favourite houseplant is a lovely way to share the joy of the indoor jungle with family and friends. There are various methods of propagation and some of the most common are outlined below. The best potting mix or rooting medium to use for cuttings is proprietary propagation mix. You can also try dipping the tips of cuttings in rooting hormone to help aid healthy root growth. Water all newly propagated plants and keep in a warm, well-lit spot out of direct sunlight. A propagation heat mat is a useful tool when propagating tropical plants. A temperature of 18 to 21 °C is usually needed for plants to take root and this may take up to thirty days. Don't allow the mix to dry out. A homemade mini-greenhouse using a

plastic bag as a kind of 'tent' can help to maintain the high humidity needed to start plants off and reduce the need for watering (but don't allow the plants to touch the sides of this tent). When the new growth starts you can pot-on into any standard, good quality potting mix.

Stem tip cutting

Many soft-stem indoor plants such as Devil's ivy, *Philodendron*, English ivy and Spiderwort, some hard-stem plants such as Rubber plants, and larger plants such as *Monstera* and the big varieties of *Philodendron* can be propagated by taking cuttings of the growing tips. Stem cuttings are usually best done in summer. Choose a new growth with several leaves on the tip and cut just below a bud or a leaf. The ideal cutting length varies, but is generally about 5 to 10 centimetres. Remove leaves from the bottom half of the cutting and put between a third to a half of the cutting in rooting medium, using a pencil or small dibber to make a hole first, then lightly infill and press down the soil.

Leaf cuttings and plantlets

Mother-in-law's tongue, begonias and *Peperomia* can be good candidates for this method. Essentially you treat the single leaf or a part of the leaf as a cutting. Mother-in-law's tongue leaves can be cut into small sections and placed vertically in a pot of seedling mix. Entire leaves of the begonia, African violet, or *Peperomia* can be placed vertically in the mix, leaving the top half poking out. Spider plant 'plantlets' that hang off the mother plant can be detached once they have three or four leaves and planted in the same way as cuttings.

Layering

Layering involves covering part of the stem with potting mix to enable it to grow a new root system. Spider plants and English ivy can be propagated in this way, as can any plant with aerial roots, or plants with long stems and plantlets at the end of stems. Prepare a number of small pots to surround the mother plant. Bend the stems of the mother plant into the new small pots, remove any leaves and cover with soil to weigh them down. You can use a paperclip, hairpin or similar to help secure the stems. When new growth appears the original stem can be severed.

Division

Common indoor plants propagated by division include the Peace lily, many ferns, some succulent and cacti, *Calathea*, *Ctenanthe* and *Cymbidium* orchids. Divide most plants in spring or summer. Prepare two pots with a good drainage layer then potting mix. Ensure the potting mix is thoroughly wet before and after division to prevent shock. Remove the plant from its original pot and remove a good lot of the potting mix around its roots using chopsticks, a dibber or garden fork. Gently pull the roots and stems apart with your hands then repot the separate sections into the different pots.

Seeds

A forgotten art in many ways! Many perennial foliage plants can be grown from seed and this is a great way to add an entirely new plant to your collection. Seedlings can be raised in much the same way as vegetables or other annual seeds. Using very clean pots and sterile soil is helpful, along with good humidity and warmth. *Coleus* is cited as being very easy to propagate from seed, as are the Coffee plant and the Umbrella tree (if you can obtain seeds).

Water rooting

Many houseplants can be propagated by putting a cutting into water. These plants can be kept in water for quite some time as long as they have a little bit of light and some nutrients or they can be planted on into potting mix. Try water rooting English ivy, Devil's ivy, Heartleaf philodendron, hoya and *Syngonium*. Other interesting ones to try are begonia, *Pilea*, succulents and cactus. A clear glass vessel allows you to see the roots grow.

Take a cutting of a new growth tip as per stem cutting. Place the stem cutting in water in your vessel. Add a little liquid fertiliser and some horticultural charcoal if you have it. Charcoal helps to 'sweeten' or purify the water. Check regularly to ensure that the water is topped up and the cut end remains submerged. Your water cutting should live for quite some time, or you might choose to plant it out after the roots develop. Plant it initially into a small pot in a mix of horticultural sand or propagating mix (it will need good sterile soil and excellent drainage to get used to being in soil) and then into normal potting mix once it is established.

There are also some common food plants or seeds to try propagating in water as indoor plants, a classic being the avocado. Simply clean off the avocado pip, insert two toothpicks in the side and suspend the pointy end up over a jar of clean water, making sure that the bottom half is always submerged. The avocado seed should sprout in around 4–6 weeks and will continue to grow for many months before needing to be potted on into soil. You can keep the avocado tree inside in a bright light as an indoor plant (although it will rarely get enough light to enable fruiting indoors). Other foods to try propagating in water are sweet potato tubers, carrot tops and pineapple tops. Unroasted coffee seeds are another food plant to try. Use very fresh green coffee beans (which are the seed), soak in water overnight then plant directly in soil.

Troubleshooting

We have all lost one. The feeling of trepidation watching a new plant addition to your home start to show signs of unhappiness is never fun. Almost every person we have spoken to in this book has made mention of their houseplant 'hospital', often outdoors on a covered verandah. Here are some common problems and rescue tips for pulling your plant back from the brink, or preventing it from reaching the precipice in the first place.

Pollutants

In general it is good policy to keep your houseplants away from air pollutants such as cigarette smoke (Maidenhairs really don't like cigarette smoke!), fumes and fly sprays.

Pests

The best way to avoid pest infestations and other problems is to keep healthy plants. Provide them with as much humidity as you can and don't stress them out by under- or over-watering. Check regularly for any insect infestations. Be sure to quarantine any infested plants to keep your other ones healthy. A good weekly shower spray is also a great way to keep plants fresh and clean of pests, as this effectively washes the insects off the leaves and down the drain. Here are some common houseplant pests and ways to tackle them.

Scale insects

Scale insects are firm-shelled, small, brownish sucking insects that are immobile. Scale can be found feeding on leaves, petioles or stems. Infested plants become weakened or stunted and begin to die. Spores on the underside of ferns are often confused for scale. Scale can be wiped or scraped off using a soft toothbrush or sponge dampened with soapy water. Eco-oil or white oil will treat it. Also try dipping a rag in rubbing alcohol or methylated spirits, or painting same onto leaves with a paintbrush. Clean leaves with fresh water soon after. Keep up a weekly plant wash in the shower or use a thorough sponge bath or mist spray to help remove any new infestations.

Mealy bug

Mealy bugs are oval-shaped, white sap-sucking insects covered with waxy material that as a group look like white cotton web-like masses often at the junction of leaf and stem. They secrete honeydew, a syrupy substance that gives leaves a shiny appearance, but is actually sticky. A weekly plant wash in the shower or thorough sponge bath or mist spray helps to remove any new infestations. Eco-oil or white oil also treats mealy bug. Prompt action is essential in dealing with mealy bug and small infestations can be removed manually with a rag dipped in rubbing alcohol or methylated spirits, or a paintbrush or cotton swab dipped in same. Using the general homemade insecticide soap water spray (a common one is 1 tablespoon of castile soap in 1 litre of water) may also help to deal with small infestations. Clean off any sprays with clean water. Infested plants become stunted, and with severe infestations, plant parts begin to die.

Aphids

Aphids are greenish, pear-shaped, soft-bodied insects that can infest a plant. An infestation of aphids may cause the leaves to curl and wrinkle. They also secrete honeydew (see mealy bug). Infestations may go undetected until honeydew or sooty mould is observed. Aphids can cause new growth to become distorted or, in extreme cases, infested plants to become stunted. A strong shower spray will help wash the aphids off the plant. You can also try spraying with homemade garlic spray (several cloves of crushed garlic mixed with water in a spray bottle). Pyrethrum sprays also treat aphids.

Red spider mite

Red spider mites are tiny, eight-legged mites barely visible without a magnifying glass. Look out for speckled yellowing or browning of leaves and stems. Close up, a silken looking web may be visible. Mites like dry air, so keep your plant's air humid and temperature comfortable. Remove affected foilage as soon as possible. A weekly water spray or sponge bath for the leaves helps avoid trouble with this pest. If infestation occurs try washing leaves with a homemade soap spray of 1 tablespoon castile soap to 1 litre of water. Clean off spray with clean water a few hours later. Badly infested plants will need to be discarded.

Fungus gnats

Fungus gnats are small flies that infest potting mix. Smaller than common house flies, they are weak fliers, usually lingering near potting mix or other organic matter. The larvae spin webs on the soil surface resembling spider webs. Adult flies can breed and emerge from potting mix and be annoying indoors although not particularly harmful to either plants or humans. In large quantities fungal gnat larvae can damage roots and stunt growth so it is best to try and get rid of them. Fungus gnats are best treated at larvae stage. Reduce any

excess moisture around your plants and do not over-water. Let your plant dry out between watering. Remove any decaying organic matter such as dead leaves from plants as this is what they feed on. Sticky fly traps such as yellow tape fly traps available at most nursery supply stores can help collect and kill off adult flies and I have heard that chunks of potato in the potting mix can be a good trap for larvae. Place a potato on potting mix with the cut side down, wait for larvae to transfer onto it and dispose of it. Repeat as necessary.

Root rot

Yellowing leaves on a plant and severe ill health with no other apparent problems may be caused by root rot. The cause is over-watering. Deprived of oxygen, the plant's roots die and rot away. To check for root rot, remove the plant from the soil and feel its roots. Affected roots will look black and feel mushy and may literally fall off the plant when touched. Healthy roots may be black or pale, but they will feel firm and pliable. Root rot can spread to other roots so needs to be treated quickly. Remove the plant from the pot and wash away and dispose of all soil from the roots. Trim away all infected roots with a sharp knife or pruners. Also trim off up to one-third of the plant's leaves to allow it to focus its energies on regrowth. Clean the pot thoroughly using natural bleach. Repot in fresh potting soil and be sure not to over-water. Do not fertilise again until the plant is showing signs of growing.

Chlorosis (yellowing leaves)

Sometimes old leaves yellow and fall off this is a normal life cycle of plants. However, ongoing, uniformly yellow foliage is a sign of chlorosis, which can be caused by all kinds of stresses including nutrient deficiency (especially iron, magnesium and zinc), poor drainage, damaged or compacted roots, root rot, temperature extremes, too much light, too little water or too much water, pest infestation or disease. Diagnosis is key here. With severe chlorosis, the leaf veins will turn yellow, followed by the death of the leaf, dying back of the stem and finally death of the entire plant.

Most commonly stress is caused by over or under-watering. Check and adjust your watering regime. Make sure the potting mix is aerated and allow it to dry right out if it is too wet. Also try flushing out the potting mix to reduce any built up alkalinity in the soil. Check for any insect infestations and treat accordingly. If the plant is in very bright light, relocate it to a position with more filtered light. Make sure it is not subject to temperature extremes. If there is no improvement, try repotting into fresh potting mix (checking for compacted root or root rot at the same time). To identify nutrient deficiency do a soil ph test and/or observe leaf discolouration. Iron chlorosis starts on younger leaves and later works inward to older leaves. Manganese and zinc deficiencies develop on inner or older leaves and then progress outward. Feed with high nitrogen and/or iron/trace element fertiliser depending on which nutrient is lacking.

Browning leaves

Browning leaves is most often 'leaf burn' caused by poor watering habits, over-watering or under-watering, problems with the quality of water, or lack of humidity in the air. Scorching from the sun is also a potential cause. Remove from any direct harsh sun and follow the tips on watering and maintaining humidity. Browned or dead leaves may be removed by making a sharp cut at the base of the leaf stem.

Wilting leaves

Wilting leaves are caused by over or under-watering, or by root rot. Check the potting mix. Allow it to dry right out if it is too moist, or give it a good soak in a bucket of water if it is bone dry. If the plant doesn't improve check for root rot.

Straggly and generally unhealthy looking leaves

Straggly and generally unhealthy looking leaves are most likely caused by not enough light. Try moving the plant closer to a natural light source. This often happens with Devil's ivy or Heartleaf philodendron placed too far from a window.

Plant index

Plants are classified using the science of taxonomy. Family, genus and species names are generally in Latin or are Latinised words from other languages, particularly Greek. Each species is assignable to a genus, each genus to a family, etc. (Note: when a name has already been mentioned it is common to abbreviate it, for example the species *Philodendron hederaceum* becomes *P. Hederaceum*.)

In this book the species name is the most often used Latin name (we also list the family name for each of the top ten plants). Overall, I have used common names throughout the text with a cross reference to the Latin (species) names in this index. Common names used are those judged commonly used in Australia. Where a general or non-specific reference to a group of plants is made within an interview, or identified in a photo caption, for example some *Philodendrons*, or succulents and the specific plant cannot be identified we give it the generic (genus) name. Where exact species cannot be identified (sometimes there are hundreds of species all very similar) we note the genus name.

Taxonomic example

The popular *Philodendron* plants referred to throughout the text are from a large family called Araceae which has multiple genus of which one is *Philodendron* and then multiple *Philodendron* species within the *Philodendron* genus.

For example: Heartleaf philodendron Family: Araceae, Genus: *Philodendron*, Species: *Philodendron hederaceum* (abbreviated to *P. hederaceum*), Common name: Heartleaf

Plants listed by common name then species name (where multiple common names, less common in Australia in brackets).

A note on accuracy

The history of botanical classification and nomenclature is complex and at times contentious, with accepted names shifting over time as more becomes known about each plant. I have used the most recently accepted name according to *The Plant List* (the result of a collaboration between the Royal Botanic Gardens, Kew and Missouri Botanical Garden). However, I am neither a botanist nor an expert in plant taxonomy. Hence there may be errors in both identification of correct species and accepted names. I have simply tried my best within the context of a (interested) layperson's knowledge and I will always welcome advice and corrections from those more expert than I am.

Further reading

Attwood, M. (1988), *Cat's Eye*, Bloomsbury, London.

Ballard, J.G. (1984), *Empire of the Sun*, Simon & Schuster, New York.

Beckett, K. (1987), *The RHS Encyclopaedia of House Plants*, Century-Hutchinson, London.

Boyd, P.D.A. (1992), 'The Victorian fern cult in south-west Britain' in, J.M., Jermy, A.C., and Paul, A.M., 'Fern horticulture: past, present and future perspectives', pp. 33–56, *Intercept*, Andover.

Boym, S. (1994), *Common places: Mythologies of everyday life in Russia*, Harvard University Press, United States of America.

Free, M. (1979), *All About House Plants*, (revised and expanded by Marjorie J. Dietz), Doubleday, New York.

Keane, M.P. (2002), *The Art of Setting Stones & Other Writings from the Japanese Garden*, Stone Bridge Press, Berkeley, California.

Keane, M.P. (2009), *Japanese Tea Garden*, Stone Bridge Press, Berkeley, California.

Lancaster, O. (1963), *Home Sweet Homes*, Murray, London.

Longman, D. (1982), *The Care of House Plants*, Book Club Associates by arrangement with Eurobook Limited, London.

Macarthur, J. (2007), *The Picturesque: Architecture, Disgust and Other Irregularities*, Routledge, London.

Macarthur, J. (2014), *The Revenge of the Picturesque*, Lecture given at the Taubman College of Architecture and Urban Planning, The University of Michigan.

Orleans, S. (2000), *The Orchid Thief*, Ballantine Books, New York.

Orwell, G. (1956), *Keep the Aspidistra Flying*, Penguin, United Kingdom.

Radcliffe-Smith A. (1984), 'Pilea peperomioides', *Kew Magazine*, vol. 1, pp. 14–19.

'Plants Indoors'. (1952), *The Architectural Review*, May.

Tompkins, P. and Bird, C. (1973), *The Secret Life of Plants*, Harper and Row, New York.

Weisbecker, P. (2012), *Greenhouse Studies*, Nieves, Zurich.

Wolverton, B. C. (1997), *How to Grow Fresh Air*, Penguin, New York.

Wolverton, B. C. (2010), *Plants: Why You Can't Live Without Them*, Roli, New Delhi.

Wolverton, B. C. and Wolverton, J. D. (1996), 'Interior plants: their influence on airborne microbes inside energy-efficient buildings', *Journal of the MS Academy of Science*, 41 (2), pp. 99-105.